D1129577

לה' הארץ ומלואה

This book belongs to:

הראל

Leah

Hebrew Name

_____

Rank

Tzivos Hashem
792 Eastern Parkway
Brooklyn, NY 11213

ISBN: 978-1-935949-51-0

Living JEWISH

A Handbook For Life

There's always someone in charge.

At home it's your parents, in the classroom it's your teachers, and on the playing field it's your coaches. The baker runs the bakery, the librarian leads the library, and the president heads the country. But what about the entire world? Who's in charge of it all?

G-d is! Over 5,000 years ago, *Hashem (G-d)* desired a home. So He created our world—the sky, stars, grass, trees, animals, and people. He wanted a place where He would feel comfortable. Where everyone would recognize their Creator and behave according to His rules. Then the world would be perfect, just as *Hashem* imagined.

But things didn't go exactly as planned. Many people don't know that the world has a Creator. Many people don't know about the Torah, where *Hashem* outlined how He wants us to behave.

Now it's up to us to change everything. *Hashem* chose us, the Jewish People, as His army. Our mission is to conquer the world—by teaching everyone around us that *Hashem* is in charge and showing others how to behave the way He wants. When will our victory be complete? With the coming of *Mashiach* (the *Messiah*), a time when the world will once again be perfect, just as *Hashem* imagined.

This handbook offers the basic training every soldier needs. Practice the army's pledge of allegiance, the *Shema*, on page 19. Learn how to proclaim Hashem as Creator with blessings in Section 2. Read about how the world will transform in the times of *Mashiach* (page 154) and the actions you can do to bring him closer (Section 4).

With the right training, there is no limit to how much we can accomplish.

Let's use our power to conquer the world for good!

What's Inside

SECTION 1

Basic Prayers

When we pray, we fulfill our mission as soldiers, recognizing that *Hashem* (G-d) can provide for all of our needs.

Praying for What We Need
Ask Away

It is a *mitzvah* (commandment) to pray to *Hashem* for all of our needs.

Triple pray

We pray three times a day:

- *Shacharit,* the morning prayer
- *Minchah,* the afternoon prayer
- *Maariv,* the evening prayer

Stop and think

In our prayers, we concentrate on:

- Standing before the King of all kings
- Connecting to *Hashem,* feeling both love and respect
- Asking for our needs, and especially that *Mashiach* (the Messiah) come now

How?

The best way to pray is in Hebrew. The prayers that our rabbis established are worded perfectly to address the King of kings. They include our soul's feelings of love and respect for *Hashem,* along with requests for everything we may need. If praying in Hebrew isn't possible, we talk to *Hashem* in a language that will make the experience meaningful.

Where?

We can pray in any place that is clean and respectful. It is best to pray in a *shul* (synagogue), and is even better to do so together with a *minyan*—a group of at least ten men, who are over the age of *Bar Mitzvah* (13 years old).

These prayers, which we recite every day, can be found in a book called a *Siddur.*

Who?

Praying is for everyone! The prayers of children are especially precious to *Hashem.* Start by learning the letters of the Hebrew alphabet, then some of the basic daily prayers.

Boys, be sure you are wearing a *kipah* on your head before you start your prayers.

The Aleph Bet
Let's Learn Hebrew!

This is the Hebrew alphabet, called the *Aleph Bet*. In Hebrew, we read from right to left. Look at each letter carefully. These are the exact same letters that *Hashem* used to create the world!

Notice how each letter also has a number. The *Aleph Bet* can also be used as a numbering system.

VAV 6	HEY 5	DALED 4	GIMMEL 3	VET 2	BET 2	ALEPH 1
FINAL CHAF 20	CHAF 20	KAF 20	YUD 10	TET 9	CHET 8	ZAYIN 7
AYIN 70	SAMECH 60	FINAL NUN 50	NUN 50	FINAL MEM 40	MEM 40	LAMED 30
REISH 200	KUF 100	FINAL TZADDIK 90	TZADDIK 90	FINAL FEY 80	FEY 80	PEY 80
			SAF 400	TAF 400	SIN 300	SHIN 300

CHOLAM	SH'VA	SEGOL	TZEIREI	PATACH	KAMATZ
CHATAF SEGOL	CHATAF PATACH	CHATAF KAMATZ	SHOOROOK	KOOBOOTZ	CHIRIK

Did you notice how the numbers jump from the single digits, to ten, then 20? Combine different letters to create bigger numbers.

To learn more about reading Hebrew, talk to your rabbi.

Modeh Ani
Rise and Shine

Our souls recharge while we sleep and return to us each morning. The first thing we do after waking up is thank *Hashem* for this new energy with *Modeh Ani*.

מוֹדֶה אֲנִי לְפָנֶיךָ מֶלֶךְ חַי וְקַיָּם,
שֶׁהֶחֱזַרְתָּ בִּי נִשְׁמָתִי בְּחֶמְלָה.
רַבָּה אֱמוּנָתֶךָ:

Mo-deh ani l'fanecha Melech chai v'ka-yam, she-he-chezarta bi nish-mati b'chemlah, rabah emunatecha.

WHAT DOES IT MEAN?

I give thanks before You, [G-d], the King who lives [and exists] forever, for You returned my soul to me with mercy. Your trustworthiness is great [because You return my soul each morning].

TRY IT!

Can you learn this by heart and say it every morning?

Netilat Yadayim
Wash Those Hands

Why?

After the *Modeh Ani* prayer, we are almost ready to serve *Hashem.* We first wash our hands in a special way, like the *kohanim* did before starting their service in the *Beit Hamikdash* (Holy Temple).

How?

Before getting out of bed, lift a cup of water and pour over the right hand, then the left. Repeat two additional times. (Lefties start with the left hand.)

After we wash our hands, brush our teeth, and finish getting dressed, we wash our hands again—the same way, but with the following blessing:

- -

בָּרוּךְ אַתָּה יְיָ, אֱלֹהֵינוּ מֶלֶךְ הָעוֹלָם,
אֲשֶׁר קִדְּשָׁנוּ בְּמִצְוֹתָיו,
וְצִוָּנוּ עַל נְטִילַת יָדָיִם:

Ba-ruch A-tah A-donai, Elo-haynu me-lech ha-olam, a-sher kid'sha-nu b'mitz-votav, v'tzi-vanu al netilat yada-yim.

WHAT DOES IT MEAN?

Blessed are You, L-rd, our G-d, King of the universe, who has made us holy with His commandments, and commanded us concerning the washing of the hands.

Preparing for Torah
A Special Blessing

Before beginning to learn *Torah* each day, we say the following blessing:

בָּרוּךְ אַתָּה יְיָ, אֱלֹהֵינוּ מֶלֶךְ הָעוֹלָם,
אֲשֶׁר בָּחַר בָּנוּ מִכָּל הָעַמִּים,
וְנָתַן לָנוּ אֶת תּוֹרָתוֹ. בָּרוּךְ אַתָּה יְיָ,
נוֹתֵן הַתּוֹרָה:

Ba-ruch Atah A-donai, Elo-haynu Melech ha-olam, asher bachar banu mi-kol ha-amim, v'natan lanu et Torato. Ba-ruch Atah A-donai, no-tayn ha-Torah.

WHAT DOES IT MEAN?

Blessed are You, L-rd, our G-d, King of the universe, who has chosen us from among all the nations and given us His Torah. Blessed are You, L-rd, who gives the Torah.

Immediately after this blessing, say some words of Torah, like the verse on the next page.

Torah
Our Greatest Gift

Every day we remind ourselves of the great treasure *Hashem* has given us: the *Torah!*

תּוֹרָה צִוָּה לָנוּ מֹשֶׁה
מוֹרָשָׁה קְהִלַּת יַעֲקֹב:

**Torah tzivah lanu Moshe
mo-rashah k'hilat Yaakov.**

WHAT DOES IT MEAN?

*The Torah that Moses commanded us
is the heritage of the Jewish congregation.*

Harayni
Lots of Love

Before we begin the *Shacharit* prayer each morning, we commit to *Hashem*—and ourselves—to love others as we love ourselves. Just like we overlook our own faults and see the good in ourselves, we can do the same for fellow Jews. When *Hashem* sees how much we care about each other, He will surely show the same love toward us, accepting our requests and showering us with blessings.

הֲרֵינִי מְקַבֵּל עָלַי מִצְוַת עֲשֵׂה שֶׁל
וְאָהַבְתָּ לְרֵעֲךָ כָּמוֹךָ:

**Harayni m'kabayl a-lai mitzvat a-say shel
v'ahavta l'ray-a-cha ka-mocha.**

WHAT DOES IT MEAN?

I hereby take upon myself to fulfill the mitzvah, "love your fellow as yourself."

The Shema
Our Pledge of Allegiance

It is a *mitzvah* to recite the *Shema* prayer every morning and night. The *Shema* has always been the anthem of the Jewish people. In it, we declare that *Hashem* is the only One who rules the heavens and the earth. This is a main principle of Jewish belief.

When saying the first line of *Shema*, we cover our eyes with our right hand so that we won't get distracted, and we can focus on the meaning of each word. *Shema* reminds us to love *Hashem* and to fulfill His *mitzvot*. The *Shema* prayer has three parts. Start by learning the first part by heart. You can find the complete prayer in a *Siddur*.

- -

שְׁמַע יִשְׂרָאֵל, יְיָ אֱלֹהֵינוּ, יְיָ אֶחָד:

בָּרוּךְ שֵׁם כְּבוֹד מַלְכוּתוֹ לְעוֹלָם וָעֶד:

וְאָהַבְתָּ אֵת יְיָ אֱלֹהֶיךָ, בְּכָל לְבָבְךָ, וּבְכָל נַפְשְׁךָ, וּבְכָל מְאֹדֶךָ: וְהָיוּ הַדְּבָרִים הָאֵלֶּה אֲשֶׁר אָנֹכִי מְצַוְּךָ הַיּוֹם, עַל לְבָבֶךָ: וְשִׁנַּנְתָּם לְבָנֶיךָ וְדִבַּרְתָּ בָּם, בְּשִׁבְתְּךָ בְּבֵיתֶךָ וּבְלֶכְתְּךָ בַדֶּרֶךְ, וּבְשָׁכְבְּךָ, וּבְקוּמֶךָ: וּקְשַׁרְתָּם לְאוֹת עַל יָדֶךָ, וְהָיוּ לְטֹטָפֹת בֵּין עֵינֶיךָ: וּכְתַבְתָּם עַל מְזֻזוֹת בֵּיתֶךָ, וּבִשְׁעָרֶיךָ:

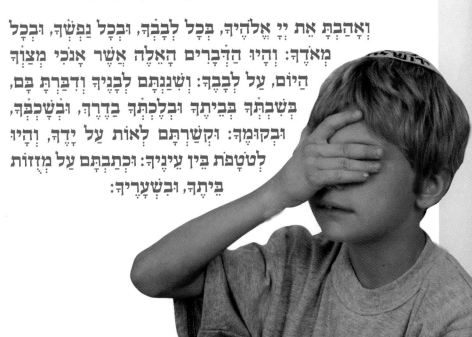

SHEMA YISRAEL, A-DONAI ELO-HAYNU, A-DONAI ECHAD.

Say the following line in an undertone:
Ba-ruch Shaym k'vod mal-chuto l'olam va-ed.

V'ahavta ayt A-donai Elo-hecha, b'chol l'vav'cha, uv-chol naf-sh'cha, uv-chol m'odecha. V'ha-yu ha-d'varim ha-ay-leh asher Anochi m'tzav'cha ha-yom, al l'va-vecha. V'shinan-tam l'va-necha v'dibarta bam, b'shiv-t'cha b'vay-techa, uv-lech-t'cha vaderech, uv-shoch-b'cha, uv-kumecha. Uk-shartam l'ot al yadecha, v'ha-yu l'totafot bayn aynecha. Uch-tavtam al m'zuzot bay-tech a, uvish-arecha.

WHAT DOES IT MEAN?

[Every] Jew [should] listen [and understand that] the L-rd is our G-d, [and that] the L-rd is [the] One [and only Ruler and King in the seven heavens, the earth, and the four corners of the universe].

The name of [G-d's] glorious kingdom is blessed forever and ever.

You should love the L-rd, your G-d, [and keep His commandments] with all of your heart, [as one does when fulfilling his beloved's request. Love G-d] with all of your soul. [Be ready to fulfill all of His commandments, even if you might lose your life. Love G-d] with all of your might. [Be ready to fulfill all of His commandments, even if you might lose your money.] These words [of Torah], which I command you [to do] today [,and every day, should always be new and fresh to you, and they should be engraved] on your heart; [you should always be thinking about them. You should] teach Torah to your children [and students until they know it well enough to answer any question about it]. You should [be involved in the words of Torah and] speak of them [whenever you can]: when you sit in your house, when you go on the way, when you lie down [at night], and when you get up [in the morning. These words, the words of the Shema, should be written in tefillin]. You should tie [the hand-tefillin] on your arm as a sign [to remember G-d], and [the head-]tefillin [should be put on your head, above the area] between your eyes. You should write [these words of the Shema on mezuzot, which you should put up] on the doorposts of your house and upon your gates.

The Amidah
Standing Silently

In the times of the *Beit Hamikdash* (Holy Temple), sacrifices were offered on behalf of all the people by the *kohanim* and *levi'im*. Ever since the *Beit Hamikdash* was destroyed, we can no longer bring actual offerings to *Hashem*. Instead, every Jew is able to fulfill these services by reciting a prayer called the *Amidah*.

All about Amidah

The *Amidah* is the holiest part of our daily prayers. It contains praise to *Hashem* and requests for all of our needs, both as individuals and as a nation. This prayer is repeated three times every day, during *Shacharit*, *Minchah*, and *Maariv*.

The *Amidah* is also called "*Shmoneh Esrei*," because of the 18 blessings originally included in its text.

Special days

On special days, like *Shabbat* and Jewish holidays, instead of asking for our needs, we say a special *Amidah* prayer in honor of the day, full of praise and thanks to *Hashem*.

More and more

On *Shabbat*, *Rosh Chodesh* (the first day of a Jewish month), and on Jewish holidays, we also include a fourth *Amidah* prayer called *Musaf*, which means "addition." On *Yom Kippur* we add a fifth *Amidah* prayer, called *Ne'ilah*.

Sheyibaneh
Mashiach Now

This prayer reminds us to eagerly await *Mashiach*, our redeemer, who will rebuild the *Beit Hamikdash* in Jerusalem. By doing good deeds and following *Hashem*'s commandments, we bring the end of exile closer, when the *Beit Hamikdash* will stand once more.

יְהִי רָצוֹן מִלְּפָנֶיךָ, יְיָ אֱלֹהֵינוּ וֵאלֹהֵי אֲבוֹתֵינוּ, שֶׁיִּבָּנֶה בֵּית הַמִּקְדָּשׁ בִּמְהֵרָה בְיָמֵינוּ, וְתֵן חֶלְקֵנוּ בְּתוֹרָתֶךָ:

Y'hi ra-tzon mil'fanecha, A-donai Elo-haynu v'Aylo-hay avotaynu, she-yiba-neh Bayt Ha-mikdash bim-hayrah v'yamaynu, v'tayn chelkaynu b'toratecha.

WHAT DOES IT MEAN?

May it be Your will, L-rd, our G-d and G-d of our fathers, that the Beit Hamikdash be speedily rebuilt in our days, and grant us our portion in Your Torah.

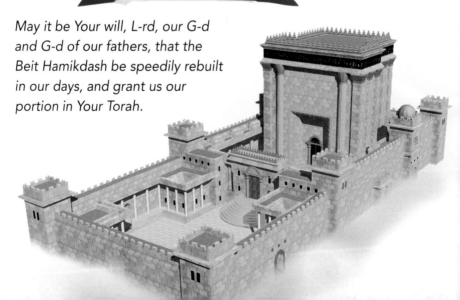

Ach Tzadikim
The Best is Yet to Come

In this prayer, we ask that there be peace for all Jews. We also ask to serve *Hashem* properly, so that we will merit to see His holiness revealed and to dwell in His presence.

אַךְ צַדִּיקִים יוֹדוּ לִשְׁמֶךָ,
יֵשְׁבוּ יְשָׁרִים אֶת פָּנֶיךָ:

**Ach tzadikim yodu lish-mecha
yay-sh'vu y'sharim et panecha.**

WHAT DOES IT MEAN?

*Indeed, the righteous will extol Your Name;
the upright will dwell in Your presence.*

SECTION 2

Blessings

Every time we make a *brachah* (blessing), we further the mission of Tzivos Hashem: make known that everything in the world belongs to it's creator, *Hashem* (G-d).

BLESSINGS

All the Brachot We Say
Bless You!

Before we eat or drink, and before doing certain *mitzvot* (commandments), we say a *brachah*. Saying a *brachah* before and after we eat is like saying, "may I please have some?" and "thank you!" By making a *brachah*, we acknowledge that *Hashem* is the Creator and Ruler of the world.

Take three

There are three general categories of *brachot* (blessings):

- *Brachot* of pleasure: We say these blessings before eating, drinking, or smelling certain fragrances

- *Brachot* for *mitzvot*: We say these blessings before performing commandments, like washing our hands, lighting *Shabbat* candles, or blowing the *shofar* (ram's horn) on *Rosh Hashanah*

- *Brachot* of thanks: We say these blessings as a special "Thank you!" to *Hashem* for giving us something special or for watching over us

TRY IT!

When we say "Amen" ("so be it") after hearing a brachah, we affirm its truth—and keep a mitzvah (commandment) at the same time!

Brachot for Food
Bon Appetit

Doing it right

Here's how to make a *brachah*:

- Check for clean hands

- Make sure that the food is ready to be eaten right away (peeled or unwrapped)

- Mouths should be empty of any other food

- Righties hold the food in their right hands; lefties in their left hands

- Boys cover their heads when saying a *brachah*

- Shh…! No talking between making the *brachah* and taking that first bite

When practicing a *brachah*, pronounce *Hashem*'s name as "*Hashem Elo-kaynu*," instead of "*Ado-nai Elo-haynu*," so as not to say His holy name when it is not needed.

Different kinds of foods have different *brachot*. Try to learn what they mean and memorize them in Hebrew. Then you will be able to say the correct *brachot* on everything that you eat!

הַמוֹצִיא · Hamotzi
Bread

Before eating a meal with bread, we wash our hands by pouring water from a washing cup. We first pour over our right hand three times, then over our left hand three times (or, if you are a lefty, in the opposite order). We then say the following:

בָּרוּךְ אַתָּה יְיָ, אֱלֹהֵינוּ מֶלֶךְ הָעוֹלָם,
אֲשֶׁר קִדְּשָׁנוּ בְּמִצְוֹתָיו וְצִוָּנוּ
עַל נְטִילַת יָדָיִם:

**Ba-ruch Atah A-donai, Elo-haynu
Me-lech ha-olam, a-sher kid'sha-nu
b'mitz-votav, v'tzi-vanu
al n'ti-lat ya-da-yim.**

WHAT DOES IT MEAN?

Blessed are You, L-rd, our G-d, King of the universe, who has made us holy us with His commandments and commanded us concerning the washing of the hands.

Next, before eating the bread, we say:

- -

בָּרוּךְ אַתָּה יְיָ, אֱלֹהֵינוּ מֶלֶךְ הָעוֹלָם,
הַמּוֹצִיא לֶחֶם מִן הָאָרֶץ:

**Ba-ruch Atah A-donai, Elo-haynu Melech
ha-olam, hamo-tzi le-chem min ha-aretz.**

WHAT DOES IT MEAN?

*Blessed are You, L-rd, our G-d, King of the universe,
Who brings forth bread from the ground.*

Mezonot · מְזוֹנוֹת
Five Grains

Before eating cake, cookies, pasta, or other non-bread foods made from wheat and other grains (barley, oat, rye, spelt), we say:

בָּרוּךְ אַתָּה יְיָ, אֱלֹהֵינוּ מֶלֶךְ הָעוֹלָם,
בּוֹרֵא מִינֵי מְזוֹנוֹת:

Ba-ruch Atah A-donai, Elo-haynu Melech ha-olam, boray minay mezonot.

WHAT DOES IT MEAN?

Blessed are You, L-rd, our G-d, King of the universe, who creates various kinds of food.

Hagafen · הַגֶּפֶן
Wine and Grape Juice

Before drinking wine or grape juice, we say:

- -

בָּרוּךְ אַתָּה יְיָ, אֱלֹהֵינוּ מֶלֶךְ הָעוֹלָם,
בּוֹרֵא פְּרִי הַגָּפֶן:

**Ba-ruch Atah A-donai,
Elo-haynu Melech ha-olam,
boray p'ri hagafen.**

WHAT DOES IT MEAN?

*Blessed are You, L-rd,
our G-d, King of the
universe, Who creates
fruit of the vine.*

Ha-aytz · הָעֵץ
Fruits

Before eating produce that grows on trees, we say:

בָּרוּךְ אַתָּה יְיָ, אֱלֹהֵינוּ מֶלֶךְ הָעוֹלָם,
בּוֹרֵא פְּרִי הָעֵץ:

**Ba-ruch Atah A-donai, Elo-haynu Melech
ha-olam, boray p'ri ha-aytz.**

WHAT DOES IT MEAN?

*Blessed are You, L-rd, our G-d, King of the universe,
Who creates fruit of the tree.*

Ha'adamah · הָאֲדָמָה
Vegetables

Before eating produce that
grows from the ground,
we say:

בָּרוּךְ אַתָּה יְיָ, אֱלֹהֵינוּ מֶלֶךְ הָעוֹלָם,
בּוֹרֵא פְּרִי הָאֲדָמָה:

**Ba-ruch Atah A-donai, Elo-haynu Melech
ha-olam, boray p'ri ha'adamah.**

WHAT DOES IT MEAN?

*Blessed are You, L-rd, our G-d, King of the universe,
who creates fruit of the earth.*

Shehakol · שֶׁהַכֹּל
Everything Else

Some foods don't fall into the other blessing categories. Before eating anything else, like fish, meat, poultry, dairy products, candy, chocolate, juice, or drinks (besides wine or grape juice), we say:

בָּרוּךְ אַתָּה יְיָ אֱלֹהֵינוּ מֶלֶךְ הָעוֹלָם
שֶׁהַכֹּל נִהְיָה בִּדְבָרוֹ:

Ba-ruch Atah A-donai, Elo-haynu Melech ha-olam, shehakol nih-yah bid-varo.

WHAT DOES IT MEAN?

Blessed are You, L-rd, our G-d, King of the universe, by Whose word all things came to be.

Concluding Blessings

Birkat Hamazon · בִּרְכַּת הַמָּזוֹן
Grace After Meals

After eating bread (on which we say the blessing of *hamotzi*), we say *Birkat Hamazon*, the Grace After Meals, to thank *Hashem* for providing us with all of our needs. Start learning the first paragraph of *Birkat Hamazon* today!

בָּרוּךְ אַתָּה יְיָ אֱלֹהֵינוּ מֶלֶךְ הָעוֹלָם,
הַזָּן אֶת הָעוֹלָם כֻּלּוֹ בְּטוּבוֹ בְּחֵן בְּחֶסֶד
וּבְרַחֲמִים הוּא נוֹתֵן לֶחֶם לְכָל בָּשָׂר
כִּי לְעוֹלָם חַסְדּוֹ: וּבְטוּבוֹ הַגָּדוֹל עִמָּנוּ
תָּמִיד לֹא חָסֵר לָנוּ וְאַל יֶחְסַר לָנוּ מָזוֹן
לְעוֹלָם וָעֶד: בַּעֲבוּר שְׁמוֹ הַגָּדוֹל כִּי הוּא
אֵל זָן וּמְפַרְנֵס לַכֹּל וּמֵטִיב לַכֹּל וּמֵכִין
מָזוֹן לְכָל בְּרִיּוֹתָיו אֲשֶׁר בָּרָא, כָּאָמוּר,
פּוֹתֵחַ אֶת יָדֶךָ וּמַשְׂבִּיעַ לְכָל חַי רָצוֹן:
בָּרוּךְ אַתָּה יְיָ הַזָּן אֶת הַכֹּל:

TRY IT!

You can find the complete text in a *Siddur* (prayerbook).

Ba-ruch Atah
A-donai, Elo-haynu
Melech ha-olam, ha-zan
et ha-olam kulo b'tuvo
b'chayn b'chesed
uv-rachamim. Hu notayn
le-chem l'chol basar, ki l'olam
chasdo. Uv-tuvo ha-gadol imanu tamid lo
chasayr lanu v'al yech-sar lanu mazon l'olam
va-ed. Ba-avur Sh'mo ha-gadol, ki Hu Ayl zan
um-farnays lakol, umaytiv lakol umay-chin
mazon l'chol b'riyotav asher bara. Ka-amur,
po-tay-ach et yadecha, umasbi-a l'chol chai
ra-tzon. Ba-ruch Atah A-donai,
ha-zan et ha-kol.

WHAT DOES IT MEAN?

*Blessed are You, L-rd, our G-d, King of the universe,
[Who,] in His goodness, provides food for the entire
world with graciousness, with kindness, and with mercy.
He gives food to all [of the world's] creations, because
His kindness lasts forever. Through His great goodness,
[which is] always with us, we do not lack [food], and may
we never lack food. [G-d gives the world food] because
of His great name; because He is the G-d Who provides
food and livelihood to everyone. [He] does good to
everyone and [He] prepares food for all of His creations;
[for everything] that He created, as it says [in Psalms]:
You open Your hand [and give enough food] to satisfy
the desires of every living thing. Blessed are You, L-rd,
Who provides food for everyone.*

Brich Rachamanah · בְּרִיךְ רַחֲמָנָא
A Child's Thanks

Young children who find it hard to say the full *Birkat Hamazon* may recite a shortened version:

בְּרִיךְ רַחֲמָנָא אֱלָהָנָא, מַלְכָּא דְעָלְמָא,
מָרָא דְהַאי פִּיתָא:

**B'rich Rachamana, Ela-hana, Malka d'al'ma,
Mara d'hai pita.**

WHAT DOES IT MEAN?

Blessed are You, L-rd, our G-d, King of the universe, Master of this bread.

Me'ayn Shalosh · מֵעֵין שָׁלֹשׁ
Threefold Blessing

After eating certain foods outside of a meal with bread, we say a special blessing.

There are three versions for the three different categories of foods:

- Cooked, fried, or baked foods made from the five grains—wheat, barley, rye, oat, or spelt
- Wine or grape juice
- Special fruits with which Israel is blessed: grapes, figs, pomegranates, olives, and dates

בָּרוּךְ אַתָּה יְיָ, אֱלֹהֵינוּ מֶלֶךְ הָעוֹלָם,

After grapes, figs, pomegranates, olives, or dates:	After wine or grape juice:	After food made from the five grains:
(וְ)עַל הָעֵץ וְעַל פְּרִי הָעֵץ	(וְ)עַל הַגֶּפֶן וְעַל פְּרִי הַגֶּפֶן	עַל הַמִּחְיָה וְעַל הַכַּלְכָּלָה

וְעַל תְּנוּבַת הַשָּׂדֶה וְעַל אֶרֶץ חֶמְדָּה טוֹבָה וּרְחָבָה שֶׁרָצִיתָ
וְהִנְחַלְתָּ לַאֲבוֹתֵינוּ לֶאֱכוֹל מִפִּרְיָהּ וְלִשְׂבּוֹעַ מִטּוּבָהּ.
רַחֵם נָא יְיָ אֱלֹהֵינוּ עַל יִשְׂרָאֵל עַמֶּךָ וְעַל יְרוּשָׁלַיִם עִירֶךָ
וְעַל צִיּוֹן מִשְׁכַּן כְּבוֹדֶךָ וְעַל מִזְבְּחֶךָ וְעַל הֵיכָלֶךָ.
וּבְנֵה יְרוּשָׁלַיִם עִיר הַקֹּדֶשׁ בִּמְהֵרָה בְיָמֵינוּ וְהַעֲלֵנוּ לְתוֹכָהּ.
וְשַׂמְּחֵנוּ בָהּ וּנְבָרֶכְךָ בִּקְדֻשָּׁה וּבְטָהֳרָה:

	On Shabbat:
On Rosh Hashanah:	וּרְצֵה וְהַחֲלִיצֵנוּ בְּיוֹם הַשַּׁבָּת הַזֶּה:
וְזָכְרֵנוּ לְטוֹבָה בְּיוֹם הַזִּכָּרוֹן הַזֶּה:	On Rosh Chodesh:
On Sukkot:	וְזָכְרֵנוּ לְטוֹבָה בְּיוֹם רֹאשׁ הַחֹדֶשׁ הַזֶּה:
וְזָכְרֵנוּ לְטוֹבָה בְּיוֹם חַג הַסֻּכּוֹת הַזֶּה:	On Pesach:
On Shemini Atzeret:	וְזָכְרֵנוּ לְטוֹבָה בְּיוֹם חַג הַמַּצּוֹת הַזֶּה:
וְזָכְרֵנוּ לְטוֹבָה בְּיוֹם שְׁמִינִי עֲצֶרֶת הַחַג הַזֶּה:	On Shavuot:
	וְזָכְרֵנוּ לְטוֹבָה בְּיוֹם חַג הַשָּׁבֻעוֹת הַזֶּה:

כִּי אַתָּה יְיָ טוֹב וּמֵטִיב לַכֹּל וְנוֹדֶה לְךָ עַל הָאָרֶץ

After grapes, figs, pomegranates, olives, or dates:	After wine or grape juice:	After food made from the five grains:
(וְעַל) הַפֵּרוֹת:	(וְעַל) פְּרִי הַגֶּפֶן:	וְעַל הַמִּחְיָה:

בָּרוּךְ אַתָּה יְיָ, עַל הָאָרֶץ

After grapes, figs, pomegranates, olives, or dates:	After wine or grape juice:	After food made from the five grains:
(וְ) הַפֵּרוֹת:	(וְעַל) פְּרִי הַגֶּפֶן:	וְעַל הַמִּחְיָה:

Ba-ruch Atah A-donai, Elo-haynu Melech ha-olam,

After food made from the five grains:	After wine or grape juice:	After grapes, figs, pomegranates, olives, or dates:
al ha-mich-yah v'al ha-kal-kalah	(v')al ha-gefen v'al p'ri ha-gefen	(v')al ha-aytz v'al p'ri ha-aytz

v'al t'nuvat ha-sa-deh, v'al eretz chemdah tovah ur-chavah
shera-tzita v'hin-chal-ta la-avo-taynu le-echol mipir-yah v'lis-bo-a
mi-tuvah, rachem na A-donai Elo-haynu al Yisrael amecha v'al
Yerushala-yim irecha v'al Tziyon mishkan k'vodecha, v'al
miz-b'checha, v'al hay-chalecha, uv-nay Yerushala-yim ir
ha-kodesh bim-hayrah v'yamaynu v'ha-alaynu l'tochah,
v'sam'chaynu vah un-varech'cha bik-dushah uv-taharah,

On *Shabbat:*	On *Shavuot:*
ur-tzay v'ha-chali-tzaynu b'yom ha-Shabbat ha-zeh,	v'zach'raynu l'tovah b'yom chag ha-Shavu-ot ha-zeh,
On *Rosh Chodesh:*	On *Rosh Hashanah:*
v'zach'raynu l'tovah b'yom Rosh ha-chodesh ha-zeh,	v'zach'raynu l'tovah b'yom ha-zikaron ha-zeh,
On *Pesach:*	On *Sukkot:*
v'zach'raynu l'tovah b'yom chag Ha-matzot ha-zeh,	v'zach'raynu l'tovah b'yom chag ha-Sukkot ha-zeh,

On *Shemini Atzeret:*
v'zoch-raynu l'tovah b'yom shemini Atzeret ha-chag ha-zeh,

Ki Atah A-donai tov umaytiv la-kol v'no-deh l'cha al ha-aretz

After food made from the five grains:	After wine or grape juice:	After grapes, figs, pomegranates, olives, or dates:
v'al ha-mich-yah.	(v'al) p'ri ha-gafen.	(v'al) ha-payrot.

Ba-ruch Atah A-donai, al ha-aretz v'al

After food made from the five grains:	After wine or grape juice:	After grapes, figs, pomegranates, olives, or dates:
v'al ha-mich-yah.	(v'al) p'ri ha-gafen.	(v')ha-payrot.

WHAT DOES IT MEAN?

Blessed are you, L-rd, our G-d, King of the universe, for

After food made from the five grains:	After wine or grape juice:	After grapes, figs, pomegranates, olives, or dates:
the sustenance and for the nourishment.	*(and for) the vine and for the fruit of the vine.*	*(and for) the tree and for the fruit of the tree.*

For the produce of the field, and for the precious, good, and spacious land that You have graciously given as a heritage to our ancestors, to eat of its fruit and to be satiated with its goodness. Have mercy, L-rd, our G-d, on Israel, Your people, on Jerusalem, Your city, on Zion, the abode of Your glory, on Your altar, and on Your Temple. Rebuild Jerusalem, the holy city, speedily in our days, and bring us up to it and make us rejoice in it, and we will bless You in holiness and purity.

On *Shabbat:*
May it please You to strengthen us on this Shabbat day.

On *Shavuot:*
Remember us for good on this day of the Festival of Shavuot.

On *Rosh Chodesh:*
Remember us for good on this day of Rosh Chodesh.

On *Rosh Hashanah:*
Remember us for good on this Day of Remembrance.

On *Pesach:*
Remember us for good on this day of the Festival of Matzot.

On *Sukkot:*
Remember us for good on this day of the Festival of Sukkot.

On *Shemini Atzeret:*
Remember us for good on this day of Shemini Atzeret, the festival.

For You, L-rd, are good and do good to all, and we offer thanks to You for the land

After food made from the five grains:	After wine or grape juice:	After grapes, figs, pomegranates, olives, or dates:
and for the sustenance.	*(and for) the fruit of the vine.*	*(and for) the fruits.*

Blessed are You, L-rd, for the land and for

After food made from the five grains:	After wine or grape juice:	After grapes, figs, pomegranates, olives, or dates:
and for the sustenance.	*(and for) the fruit of the vine.*	*(and) the fruits.*

Boray Nefashot · בּוֹרֵא נְפָשׁוֹת
Creator of All

We say this *brachah* after eating anything on which the first blessing was *shehakol*, *ha'adamah*, or *ha'aytz* (except for the special fruits of Israel):

בָּרוּךְ אַתָּה יְיָ, אֱלֹהֵינוּ מֶלֶךְ הָעוֹלָם,
בּוֹרֵא נְפָשׁוֹת רַבּוֹת וְחֶסְרוֹנָן, עַל כֹּל
מַה שֶּׁבָּרָאתָ לְהַחֲיוֹת בָּהֶם נֶפֶשׁ כָּל חָי,
בָּרוּךְ חֵי הָעוֹלָמִים:

Ba-ruch Atah A-donai, Elo-haynu Melech ha-olam, boray nefashot rabot v'chesronan, al kol mah shebarata l'ha-cha-yot ba-hem nefesh kol chai. Ba-ruch Chay ha-olamim.

WHAT DOES IT MEAN?

Blessed are You, L-rd, our G-d, King of the universe,
Creator of numerous living beings and their needs,
for all the things You have created with which
to sustain the soul of every living being.
Blessed is He who is the life of the worlds.

Various Blessings:

There are special *brachot* to say at special times.

Something New
Granting Us Life

Something new

We say this *brachah* when lighting candles and saying the *Kiddush* prayer on holidays. We also say this blessing when eating a fruit for the first time in its season.

- -

בָּרוּךְ אַתָּה יְיָ, אֱלֹהֵינוּ מֶלֶךְ הָעוֹלָם,
שֶׁהֶחֱיָנוּ וְקִיְּמָנוּ וְהִגִּיעָנוּ לִזְמַן הַזֶּה:

Ba-ruch Atah A-donai, Elo-haynu Melech ha-olam, shehe-cheyanu v'kiy'manu v'higi-anu liz-man ha-zeh.

WHAT DOES IT MEAN?

Blessed are You, L-rd, our G-d, King of the universe, Who has granted us life, sustained us, and enabled us to reach this occasion.

Pleasant Smells
Breathe In

Before smelling fragrant spices, we say:

בָּרוּךְ אַתָּה יְיָ, אֱלֹהֵינוּ מֶלֶךְ
הָעוֹלָם, בּוֹרֵא מִינֵי בְשָׂמִים:

**Ba-ruch Atah A-donai,
Elo-haynu Melech ha-olam,
boray minay v'samim.**

WHAT DOES IT MEAN?

*Blessed are You, L-rd, our G-d,
King of the universe,
Who creates various kinds of spices.*

This *brachah* is said during the *Havdalah* ceremony at the end of *Shabbat,* a day when we are gifted with an extra *neshamah* (soul). We smell the fragrant spices as a comfort for the loss of this extra soul, which leaves us when Shabbat ends.

Havdalah Fire
Celebrating Light

This brachah is said during the *Havdalah* ceremony at the end of *Shabbat* and *Yom Kippur*, but not at the end of holidays. When looking at the light of the candle, we say:

בָּרוּךְ אַתָּה יְיָ, אֱלֹהֵינוּ מֶלֶךְ הָעוֹלָם, בּוֹרֵא מְאוֹרֵי הָאֵשׁ:

**Ba-ruch Atah A-donai,
Elo-haynu Melech ha-olam,
boray m'oray ha-aysh.**

WHAT DOES IT MEAN?

*Blessed are You, L-rd, our G-d,
King of the universe, Who creates the lights of fire.*

When the world was first created, *Hashem's* presence lit up the world at all times. After Adam and Chava (Eve) ate from the forbidden tree, *Hashem* decided to hide this light. But it was late Friday afternoon, so He waited until the end of Shabbat. As the holy day came to an end, the world was engulfed in darkness for the first time. Adam was then granted the wisdom to create fire: he struck two stones against each other and light sprang forth. It was then that this blessing was first said.

Power and Might
Storms

Everyone is awed by the sound of thunder. It makes us feel humble and reminds us of Hashem's power. When we hear thunder or see a tornado, hurricane, tsunami, or earthquake, we say the following *brachah*:

בָּרוּךְ אַתָּה יְיָ, אֱלֹהֵינוּ מֶלֶךְ הָעוֹלָם, שֶׁכֹּחוֹ וּגְבוּרָתוֹ מָלֵא עוֹלָם:

Ba-ruch Atah A-donai, Elo-haynu Melech ha-olam, shekocho ug-vurato malay olam.

WHAT DOES IT MEAN?

Blessed are You, L-rd, our G-d, King of the universe, Whose power and might fill the world.

Re-enacting Creation
Wonders in the Sky

Upon seeing lightning or shooting stars,
the following *brachah* is said:

בָּרוּךְ אַתָּה יְיָ, אֱלֹהֵינוּ מֶלֶךְ הָעוֹלָם,
עוֹשֶׂה מַעֲשֵׂה בְרֵאשִׁית:

**Ba-ruch Atah A-donai, Elo-haynu Melech
ha-olam, osay ma-asay v'ray-sheet.**

WHAT DOES IT MEAN?

*Blessed are You, L-rd, our G-d, King of the universe,
who re-enacts the works of creation.*

Covenant Reminder
Rainbows

When Noach (Noah) left the
ark after the great flood, *Hashem*
showed him a rainbow. It was a sign
that He would never again bring the same
destruction to the entire world. When we see
a rainbow, we are reminded of this and say:

בָּרוּךְ אַתָּה יְיָ, אֱלֹהֵינוּ מֶלֶךְ הָעוֹלָם, זוֹכֵר
הַבְּרִית וְנֶאֱמָן בִּבְרִיתוֹ וְקַיָם בְּמַאֲמָרוֹ:

**Ba-ruch Atah A-donai, Elo-haynu Melech
ha-olam, zochayr hab'rit v'ne-eman biv-rito
v'ka-yam b'ma-amaro.**

WHAT DOES IT MEAN?

*Blessed are You, L-rd, our G-d, King of the universe,
Who remembers the covenant, is faithful to His
covenant, and keeps His promise.*

SECTION 3

The Twelve Pesukim

The *Torah* is a soldier's book of orders.
Here are the 12 fundamental verses
that teach us how to fulfill our unique
purpose in this world.

① Torah · תּוֹרָה

תּוֹרָה צִוָּה לָנוּ מֹשֶׁה,
מוֹרָשָׁה קְהִלַּת יַעֲקֹב:

**Torah tzivah lanu Moshe,
morashah k'hilat Yaakov.**

WHAT DOES IT MEAN?

*The Torah that Moses commanded us
is the heritage of the congregation
of Jacob (Deut. 33:4).*

The *Torah* was given to us
through Moshe (Moses),
Hashem's (G-d's) most faithful
servant. This means that
every single Jew inherits
the *Torah* for themselves.
Whether we have studied
Torah for years or only
know a little bit, it is our
inheritance—the very best
present that *Hashem* gave
the Jewish people.

② Shema · שְׁמַע

שְׁמַע יִשְׂרָאֵל, יְיָ אֱלֹהֵינוּ, יְיָ אֶחָד:

**Sh'ma Yisrael, Ado-nai
Elo-haynu, Ado-nai Echad.**

WHAT DOES IT MEAN?

*Hear O Israel: the L-rd is our G-d;
the L-rd is One (Deut. 6:4).*

- -

The *Shema* teaches us that *Hashem* is
One, and that He is everywhere. This
concept is hinted to by the letters of
the Hebrew word for one, "*echad*": אחד

- א **Aleph = 1:** *Hashem* is One. He gives
  life to all creation.

- ח **Chet = 8:** He can be found in the
  seven heavens and the one earth.

- ד **Daled = 4:** He can be found in the four
  far-flung corners of the universe.

Have you ever heard this song?

Hashem is here, *Hashem* is there,
Hashem is truly everywhere. (2x)

Up, up, down, down, right, left, and all around,
here, there, and everywhere,
that's where He can be found. (2x)

③ B'chol · בְּכָל

בְּכָל דּוֹר וָדוֹר חַיָּב אָדָם לִרְאוֹת אֶת
עַצְמוֹ כְּאִלּוּ הוּא יָצָא מִמִּצְרָיִם:

**B'chol dor vador cha-yav adam lir-ot et
atzmo k'ilu hu ya-tza mimitzra-yim.**

WHAT DOES IT MEAN?

*In every generation one must look upon himself as if he
personally had gone out of Egypt (Pesachim 116b).*

- -

Some 3,300 years ago *Hashem* redeemed us from Egypt and
brought us from slavery to freedom. Had He not taken us out
of Egypt, we would still be slaves today. We thank *Hashem*
daily for our freedom, promising in our hearts to use our
liberty to serve *Him*, the King of all kings.

4 Kol · כָּל

כָּל יִשְׂרָאֵל יֵשׁ לָהֶם חֵלֶק לְעוֹלָם הַבָּא
שֶׁנֶּאֱמַר, וְעַמֵּךְ כֻּלָּם צַדִּיקִים
לְעוֹלָם יִירְשׁוּ אָרֶץ, נֵצֶר מַטָּעַי מַעֲשֵׂה
יָדַי לְהִתְפָּאֵר:

**Kol Yisrael yaysh lahem chaylek l'Olam Haba,
she-ne-emar, v'amaych kulam tzadikim
l'olam yi-r'shu aretz, naytzer ma-ta-ai ma-asay
yadai l'hitpa-ayr.**

WHAT DOES IT MEAN?

*All of Israel have a share in the World to Come. As it is
stated (Isaiah 60:21): "And Your people are all righteous.
They shall inherit the land forever. They are the branch of
My planting, the work of My hands, in which I take pride"
(Sanhedrin 90a).*

- -

Hashem is proud of each and every Jew. He created us and
cares for us, watching over us the way a gardener watches
over a tender plant. As we grow, learning His *Torah* and
doing *mitzvot* (commandments), *Hashem* prepares a place
for us in the World to Come, beside all the great Jewish
people of our history.

⑤ Ki Karov · כִּי

כִּי קָרוֹב אֵלֶיךָ הַדָּבָר מְאֹד,
בְּפִיךָ וּבִלְבָבְךָ לַעֲשׂתוֹ:

**Ki karov aylecha ha-davar m'od
b'ficha uvil-vav'cha la-a-soto.**

WHAT DOES IT MEAN?

*It is within your reach to follow the Torah in speech,
feeling, and deed (Deut. 30:14, as explained in the Tanya).*

The *Torah* is not in heaven! It's right here on earth, accessible
for us to learn and to keep. In fact, Judaism is as near as
the synagogue on the corner, the book
on the shelf, or the verse we are now
learning by heart. *Torah* is what our
souls really want—that's how
Hashem created us!

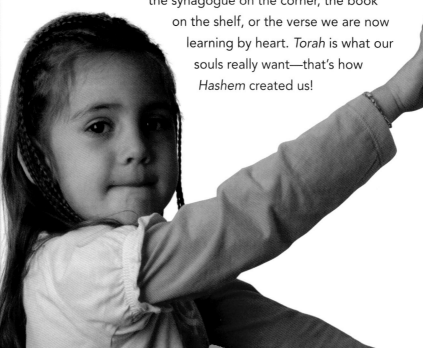

⑥ V'hinay · וְהִנֵּה

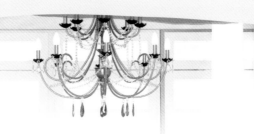

וְהִנֵּה ה' נִצָּב עָלָיו וּמָלֵא
כָּל הָאָרֶץ כְּבוֹדוֹ, וּמַבִּיט עָלָיו וּבוֹחֵן
כְּלָיוֹת וָלֵב אִם עוֹבְדוֹ כָּרָאוּי:

**V'hinay Hashem nitzav alav um-lo
chol ha-aretz k'vodo, umabit alav uvochayn
k'la-yot va-layv, im ov'do kara-uy.**

WHAT DOES IT MEAN?

*The whole earth is filled with G-d's glory. And G-d
stands over man, searching his mind and heart to see if
he is serving Him as is fitting (Tanya, Chapter 41).*

Imagine that you are in the palace of a king, surrounded
by beautiful furniture and rich decorations. You see princes
and rulers dressed in their finest clothing, hoping to catch a
glimpse of the king and waiting to carry out his command.
You pass by and suddenly find yourself…before the king!
The chamber is silent. He is looking right at you, watching
with interest as you come near. Imagine how you would feel!
This is exactly how we must feel all the time, standing before
Hashem, the King of the whole world.

⑦ B'raysheet • בְּרֵאשִׁית

בְּרֵאשִׁית בָּרָא אֱלֹהִים
אֵת הַשָּׁמַיִם וְאֵת הָאָרֶץ:

**B'ray-sheet bara Elo-kim
ayt ha-shama-yim v'ayt ha-aretz.**

WHAT DOES IT MEAN?

*In the beginning, G-d created the heavens
and the earth (Gen. 1:1).*

- -

Hashem created the whole world—the heavens, the earth, and everything in between. He gave us the *Torah*, which tells us how to live our lives and how we can make the world holy. If we ever feel frightened by darkness, a storm, or anything else, the *Torah* tells us to not be afraid. After all, *Hashem* created everything, and He is taking care of the whole world and everything inside it. When *Hashem* sees that we are doing the right thing, He sends us blessings and success.

PESUKIM

⑧ V'shinantam · וְשִׁנַּנְתָּם

וְשִׁנַּנְתָּם לְבָנֶיךָ וְדִבַּרְתָּ בָּם, בְּשִׁבְתְּךָ
בְּבֵיתֶךָ וּבְלֶכְתְּךָ בַדֶּרֶךְ וּבְשָׁכְבְּךָ וּבְקוּמֶךָ:

**V'shinan-tam l'va-necha v'dibarta bam,
b'shiv-t'cha b'vaytecha, uv-lech-t'cha
vaderech, uv-shoch-b'cha, uv-kumecha.**

WHAT DOES IT MEAN?

*And you shall teach the Torah to your children; speak of
Torah when you are home and when you travel, before
you lie down to sleep and when you awake (Deut. 6:7).*

The *Torah* tells our parents: "Pass me down to your children!
I want them to know all of my holy words." We, too, tell
our parents: "Daddy, Mommy, wouldn't you like to do the
greatest and best thing of all for me?
Please teach me *Torah*!"

⑨ Yagati · יָגַעְתִּי

יָגַעְתִּי וְלֹא מָצָאתִי
אַל תַּאֲמִין,

לֹא יָגַעְתִּי וּמָצָאתִי
אַל תַּאֲמִין,

יָגַעְתִּי וּמָצָאתִי תַּאֲמִין:

**Yaga-ti v'lo ma-tzati al ta-amin,
lo yaga-ti uma-tzati al ta-amin,
yaga-ti uma-tzati ta-amin.**

WHAT DOES IT MEAN?

*If someone says, "I have worked hard and I have not
been successful," don't believe them.
If someone says, "I have not worked hard and I have
been successful," don't believe them.
If someone says, "I have worked hard and I have been
successful," believe them (Megilla 6b).*

- -

If we did something not quite right, and we don't feel
strong enough to carry on learning *Torah* and fulfilling
mitzvot (commandments), we can remember
Hashem's promise to us: if we try harder, again,
with all of our might, then surely we will
succeed in returning to *Hashem*.

⑩ V'ahavta · וְאָהַבְתָּ

וְאָהַבְתָּ לְרֵעֲךָ כָּמוֹךָ,
רַבִּי עֲקִיבָא אוֹמֵר, זֶה כְּלָל גָּדוֹל בַּתּוֹרָה:

V'ahav-ta l'ray-acha kamocha,
Rabi Akiva omayr, zeh k'lal gadol ba-Torah.

WHAT DOES IT MEAN?

*Rabbi Akiva says that "to love your fellow as yourself"
is a great principle of the Torah
(Leviticus 19:18, Midrash).*

- -

As we try to make ourselves better people, we can't forget about helping our friends and neighbors. As Rabbi Akiva said, we must love other people just like we love ourselves. That is the main goal of our learning.

If we are lucky enough to study *Torah*, we can also help our Jewish friends learn!

11 V'zeh · וְזֶה

וְזֶה כָּל הָאָדָם וְתַכְלִית בְּרִיאָתוֹ וּבְרִיאַת
כָּל הָעוֹלָמוֹת עֶלְיוֹנִים וְתַחְתּוֹנִים, לִהְיוֹת
לוֹ דִירָה זוֹ בְּתַחְתּוֹנִים:

**V'zeh kol ha-adam v'tachlit b'ri-ato uv-ri-at
kol ha-olamot, el-yonim v'tach-tonim, lih-yot
Lo dirah zo b'tach-tonim.**

WHAT DOES IT MEAN?

*The purpose of creation is to make a dwelling
place for G-d in this world (Tanya, chap. 33).*

Hashem gave us the special job of making
ourselves and the world around us into a home for
Him. This is the reason *Hashem* created the entire
world and the Jewish people. When we follow
the *mitzvot* of the *Torah*, we are doing
our part to help build *Hashem*'s home.

12 Yismach · יִשְׂמַח

יִשְׂמַח יִשְׂרָאֵל בְּעוֹשָׂיו, פֵּירוּשׁ
שֶׁכָּל מִי שֶׁהוּא מִזֶּרַע יִשְׂרָאֵל
יֵשׁ לוֹ לִשְׂמוֹחַ בְּשִׂמְחַת ה' אֲשֶׁר
שָׂשׂ וְשָׂמֵחַ בְּדִירָתוֹ בְּתַחְתּוֹנִים:

**Yismach Yisrael b'osav, payrush
she-kol mi she-hu mi-zera Yisrael
yaysh lo lis-mo-ach b'simchat Hashem, asher
sas v'samay-ach b'dirato b'tachtonim.**

WHAT DOES IT MEAN?

*Jews rejoice in their Maker. Every Jew shares in G-d's
joy, Who rejoices and is happy in His dwelling place in
this world (Tanya, chap. 33).*

All Jews, no matter where they come from or how much they
know, are part of one nation. All Jews
can be happy and proud that *Hashem*
has given us the greatest mission: to
make ourselves, our homes,
and the world a place
where *Hashem* can feel
comfortable.

SECTION 4

Mitzvot

By doing what *Hashem* (G-d) wants, we show the world that He is in charge. He gave us, His soldiers, 613 commandments—each one brings us closer to achieving victory.

Shabbat
Make It Holy

The seventh day

The *Torah* says, "In six days, *Hashem* created the heavens and the earth. On the seventh day, He rested and made the day holy." Just like *Hashem* rested from creation, we also rest from work on the seventh day, which is called *Shabbat*. *Shabbat* is a holy time, set apart from every other day of the week. It is a day to set aside our mundane pursuits and spend time praying, learning *Torah,* and thinking about *Hashem*.

Our testimony

By keeping *Shabbat*, we demonstrate our belief that *Hashem* is the Creator and King of the whole world, and that everything in it belongs to Him.

What Hashem wants

The *Torah* tells us how to rest on *Shabbat*. From sundown on Friday until nightfall the next day we are careful not to do certain weekday activities, like use electricity, drive, write, or handle money. In fact, there are 39 different kinds of activities that the *Torah* says not to do on *Shabbat*.

TRY IT!

Attend a *Shabbat* meal! Host one in your home or ask your rabbi about a community dinner.

Shabbat Preparations
Make It Special

Cleaning

Before *Shabbat*, we prepare the house so that it reflects the day's holiness. We spread a white tablecloth over the *Shabbat* table, getting ready for our *Shabbat* feasts.

Cooking

Since cooking is not allowed on *Shabbat*, we make all the festive dishes beforehand.

Getting ready

We shower or bathe on Friday afternoon and get dressed in our nicest clothing in honor of *Shabbat*.

Shabbat Candles
Light It Up

Who?

Lighting candles in honor of *Shabbat* and holidays is one of the special *mitzvot* (commandments) for women. A girl begins lighting a candle alongside her mother at the age of three, or as soon as she is able to say the blessing. If no women or girls are present in the home, a man or boy lights the candles.

In case of emergency: if you miss the time for candle-lighting, you can still light during the 18 minutes before sunset. Once *Shabbat* has started, kindling a flame is no longer allowed.

How many?

Married women light at least two candles. Some have the custom to light an additional candle for each child in the family. Girls and single women light one candle each.

When?

Candles are lit 18 minutes before sunset. Always check a Jewish calendar for the exact lighting times for your city.

Why?

By lighting *Shabbat* candles on Friday evening, mothers and daughters bring peace, light, and holiness into their homes and into the entire world.

How?

- Before lighting, put some money into a *tzedakah* (charity) box. After lighting, it is forbidden to handle money.
- A daugther lights before her mother does, so that she can receive help as needed.
- Wave your hands three times over the candles in a welcoming motion, then cover your eyes and say the following blessing:

TRY IT!

To find out the exact time that *Shabbat* begins in your city, look in a Jewish calendar or visit *chabad.org/candlelighting* before *Shabbat* starts.

בָּרוּךְ אַתָּה יְיָ, אֱלֹהֵינוּ מֶלֶךְ הָעוֹלָם,
אֲשֶׁר קִדְּשָׁנוּ בְּמִצְוֹתָיו וְצִוָּנוּ לְהַדְלִיק
נֵר שֶׁל שַׁבָּת קֹדֶשׁ:

Ba-ruch Atah A-donai, Elo-haynu Melech ha-olam, asher kid'sha-nu b'mitz-votav, v'tzi-vanu l'hadlik nayr shel Shabbat kodesh.

WHAT DOES IT MEAN?

Blessed are You, L-rd, our G-d, King of the universe, who made us holy with His commandments, and commanded us to kindle the light of the holy Shabbat.

Celebrating Shabbat
The Grand Opening

Kiddush is a special prayer acknowledging *Hashem* as the Creator of the world. We thank Him for choosing us over the other nations of the world, redeeming us from slavery in Egypt, and giving us the *mitzvah* of keeping the *Shabbat* holy. On *Shabbat* we make *Kiddush* twice, on Friday night and on Saturday morning after prayers.

Kiddush is recited while holding a cup of wine or grape juice. We do not talk during the *Kiddush* prayer until we have drunk some of the wine or grape juice that was used to make the blessing.

The *Kiddush* prayer includes the blessing of "*hagafen*" (see page 31).

After *Kiddush* on Friday night and *Shabbat* afternoon, we eat a delicious meal. We make the blessing of *hamotzi* (see pages 28-29) on two *challot*, called *lechem mishnah*, to remind us of the double portion of manna that the Jews received in the desert every Friday, so that they would have manna for *Shabbat*.

We also eat a third meal on *Shabbat* afternoon called *Seudah Shelishit*.

Shabbat is a great time to learn and share *Torah*. It is inspiring when everyone says a *Torah* thought at the *Shabbat* table.

TRY IT!

Boys, help your father make *Kiddush* or ask for permission to make *Kiddush* yourself.

Havdalah
A New Week Begins

When three medium-sized stars appear in the sky on
Saturday night, it's time to say goodbye to the holiness of
the seventh day. Before we resume our weekday activities
(like driving or turning on lights), we listen to (or say) a
special prayer called *Havdalah*, which separates the
holiness of *Shabbat* from the rest of the week.

The *Havdalah* prayer has different parts:

- The blessing on wine or grape juice (see page 31)
- The blessing on spices (see page 44)
- The blessing on the *Havdalah* candle's light
  (see page 45)
- The *Havdalah* prayer itself

We do not talk during *Havdalah* until after the
person reciting it concludes the blessing and
drinks the wine or grape juice.

After *Havdalah* is heard all activities that were forbidden on *Shabbat* become permitted. We can then wish each other a good week by saying *"shavuah tov,"* in Hebrew, or *"a gutte voch,"* in Yiddish.

If hearing (or saying) *Havdalah* right after Shabbat isn't possible, weekday activities can be resumed after the following blessing. The complete *Havdalah* prayer must still be said or heard afterward.

DID YOU KNOW?

After *Havdalah*, it is customary to eat a special meal called a *Melaveh Malkah*, to usher out *Shabbat* with honor.

בָּרוּךְ הַמַּבְדִּיל
בֵּין קֹדֶשׁ לְחוֹל:

**Ba-ruch hamavdil
bayn kodesh l'chol.**

WHAT DOES IT MEAN?

*Blessed be He who makes
a distinction between sacred
and mundane.*

Keeping Kosher
You Are What You Eat

The *mitzvah* of *kosher* means keeping the *Torah* laws that tell us what we may and may not eat. Just like some foods can be healthy or harmful for our bodies, food also has an effect on our *neshamot* (souls). For this reason, *kosher* food is the best kind for us.

Kosher meat

For an animal to be considered *kosher*, it must be healthy, with the following signs:

- Its hooves are split
- It chews its cud

Shechitah

For meat to be *kosher* the animal must be *shechted* (ritually slaughtered), by a trained and ordained professional, according to the laws of the *Torah*, called *shechitah*.

The best kind of *kosher* meat is called *glatt kosher*. This means that after the animal is slaughtered, its lungs are carefully inspected to make sure that it was perfectly healthy.

Soaking and salting

We are not allowed to eat blood, so after the animal is slaughtered the meat is soaked, salted, and rinsed to remove all the blood.

Certification

Meat from a *kosher* animal must have *kosher* certification to ensure that it was prepared correctly.

Kosher milk

Kosher dairy products come from *kosher* animals, such as cows, goats, and sheep.

Wait on it

Meat and milk cannot be mixed or eaten during the same meal. After eating meat or poultry, we wait six hours before eating dairy foods again. After drinking milk or eating cheese, ice cream, yogurt, or other dairy foods, we wait one hour (some people wait half an hour) before eating meat.

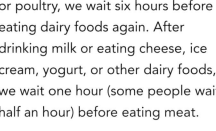

After eating aged, hard cheese we wait six hours before eating meat.

Keeping it separate

We use different cookware, dishes, and cutlery for dairy and for meat foods.

The milking of cows, goats, or sheep needs to be supervised by a Jew. This way we can be sure that no non-*kosher* milk will be mixed in. This is called *chalav Yisrael*.

If kitchenware used for dairy foods was accidentally used for meat, or vice-versa, call a rabbi right away. He can help figure out whether the dishes can become *kosher* again.

Everything else

Foods that contain neither milk nor meat are called *pareve*. These include water, fruits and vegetables, juices, grains, beans, eggs, and fish. If a *pareve* food is mixed or cooked with a meat or milk food, it has the same *kosher* status as the food with which it is mixed.

Insects

Insects are not *kosher*. Before eating fruits or vegetables, especially those where bugs are commonly found (such as dates or lettuce), we check carefully to be sure that there are no insects.

Fish

To be *kosher*, fish must
have two signs:

- Fins
- Scales

Unlike animals and birds, fish do not have
to be *shechted* or salted. Salmon, tuna, and carp are all
examples of *kosher* fish. Catfish, sharks, eels and shellfish—
like clams, oysters, shrimp, and lobster—are not *kosher*.

Fowl

The *Torah* tells us which birds we can
and cannot eat. Some examples of
kosher birds are chickens, turkeys,
ducks, geese, and doves. Some
examples of non-*kosher* birds are
hawks, owls, vultures, and eagles.

Poultry

Kosher poultry is slaughtered using
the *shechitah* method, and then it is
soaked and salted.

Eggs

We may only eat eggs from *kosher*
birds. Because it is forbidden to eat blood, eggs must be
checked for blood spots before we can
cook with them. If we find a spot
of blood in an egg, we throw
it away.

Eating out

A restaurant is *kosher* if it has a reliable *kosher* certificate on display, has a *mashgiach*, and is closed on *Shabbat*.

Shopping kosher

When shopping for food, look for a *kosher* symbol on the package. The symbol certifies that a food contains only *kosher* ingredients and that its production has been carefully overseen by a trained *kosher* supervisor, called a *mashgiach*.

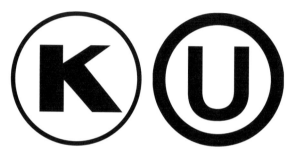

These are just two of the many kosher symbols out there. Talk to your local rabbi about which certifications are good to use.

CAUTION!
A letter "K" on a food label by itself may not necessarily mean that the food is *kosher*. The company might be claiming that their food is *kosher* without having a rabbi certify it. Make sure to look for reliable *kosher* signs, like the ones shown on this page.

TRY IT!

How many different *kosher* labels can you collect? How many *kosher* restaurants are nearby?

Tzedakah
Give It Up

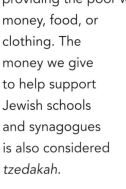

"*Tzedakah*" (charity) is about doing the right thing by helping those in need. We can fulfill this *mitzvah* by inviting guests, visiting the sick, teaching others, or providing the poor with money, food, or clothing. The money we give to help support Jewish schools and synagogues is also considered *tzedakah*.

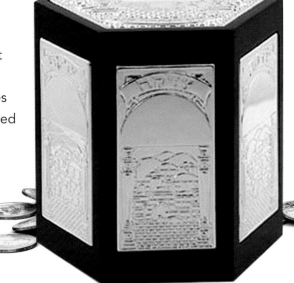

DID YOU KNOW?
It is a Jewish custom to give money to *tzedakah* every day before praying. Since we don't handle money on *Shabbat* and *yomim tovim* (holidays), we give an extra portion of *tzedakah* before candle-lighting.

How much?

We give at least a tenth of our earnings to *tzedakah*, a practice called *maaser*. Of course, giving more than that amount is even better. Remember, donating to *tzedakah* does not diminish our wealth—*Hashem* rewards us for every penny that we give.

How to give

We give *tzedakah* generously and with a smile, demonstrating how glad we are to have the chance to help another Jew. Here are the eight ways to give, as outlined in Jewish law, starting with the most ideal way:

1. Providing a job or loan to someone so that they will not have to take *tzedakah* from others.

2. Giving when you don't know who is receiving and the receiver doesn't know who is giving. (*Example: Putting money in a tzedakah box so that a poor person can receive without being embarrassed.*)

3. Giving to someone without letting them find out who the *tzedakah* is coming from. (*Example: Leaving money on a poor person's doorstep.*)

4. Giving to others who know where the charity is coming from while you don't know where it's going. (*Example: Leaving food on your doorstep for poor people to take.*)

5. Giving before being asked.

6. Giving a generous amount after being asked.

7. Giving an average amount after being asked.

8. Giving any amount of money with a bad attitude.

When we give generously to the poor, *Hashem* is generous with us. He provides us with our needs, answers our prayers, and grants us long lives. Giving *tzedakah* also brings *Mashiach* (the Messiah) closer.

DID YOU KNOW?
The *mitzvah* of *tzedakah* is unique because it can be fulfilled unknowingly. If you accidentally lose a coin and a poor person finds it, you have fulfilled the *mitzvah* of *tzedakah*.

Kibbud Av V'eim
Honoring Our Parents

The *mitzvah* of honoring our parents, called *kibbud av v'eim,* is very important—it is one of the Ten Commandments. By honoring our fathers and mothers, we are also honoring *Hashem,* because He chose our parents as His partners in bringing us into the world. *Hashem* promises that the reward for being careful with this *mitzvah* is a long life.

Getting in the habit

Here are some ways we can keep this *mitzvah:*

- Listen to our parents, quickly and happily doing what they ask, even when it is difficult for us

- Don't contradict our parents, even if we disagree with them, and hear their views before respectfully sharing our opinions

- If someone asks a question in a public setting, wait for our parents to answer before we do

- Don't sit in our parents' seats

- Thank our parents for the good things they do for us and express how grateful we are for all the work they do to provide us with food, clothing, and an education

- Call or write to our parents whenever we are away from home

Just like we need to respect our parents, we must also show respect for stepparents, grandparents, teachers, and any older people (even brothers and sisters).

Your Kid
Camp

Mom and Dad
123 Home Dr.
My Town, NC 27615

TRY IT!

Write your parents a letter expressing gratitude for all that they do.

Ahavat Yisrael
True Friendship

All people must be treated respectfully and fairly, yet the relationship between fellow Jews is special.

The Jewish people are compared to one body in which every part is essential. If one Jew is missing, the "body" is not complete; each of us is a vital part of a larger whole.

The Baal Shem Tov (founder of *Chassidut*) said that the purpose of a person's entire life may be to do just one favor for a fellow Jew.

Hashem loves each and every Jew as His only child. Since we are all *Hashem*'s children, we share the same Father—and that makes all of us like real brothers and sisters!

Golden Rule

Ahavat Yisrael means loving your fellow Jew. Rabbi Akiva said that this *mitzvah* is a major principle of the *Torah*. When the great sage Hillel was asked to teach the entire *Torah* while standing on one foot, he said, "The main point of the *Torah* is, 'Don't do to others what you would not like done to you!'" Before interacting with another person, stop and think: *how would I want to be treated?*

How to love

We can fulfill the *mitzvah* of *Ahavat Yisrael* by doing acts of kindness, such as:

- Sticking up for people when they need help
- Visiting the sick or elderly
- Writing to friends, parents, or relatives
- Sharing our belongings
- Not speaking negatively about other people
- Not listening to rumors or gossip
- Teaching *Torah* to those who know less than we do
- Including others in games and social outings

TRY IT!

What are some other ways that you can fulfill the *mitzvah* of *Ahavat Yisrael?*

Learning Torah
Everyday Growth

Learning *Torah* is not like studying any other subject. G-d's deepest wisdom is contained inside its words. By studying *Torah*, we connect with G-d's very essence!

After praying, be sure to start off each day with words of *Torah*.

It is a *mitzvah* for every Jew, young and old, to learn *Torah* whenever they can.

The word "*Torah*" also means "teachings." Every part of *Torah* shows us how to become our best selves and make the world a better place.

Getting started

Before beginning to learn *Torah* each day, say the blessing found on page 16.

Make *Torah* study a habit! Set aside a time that works, remove any distractions, and stay committed to your schedule.

Find a friend or rabbi who will become your study partner. Two heads are better than one, and learning with someone else can motivate you to keep up the practice.

The Mezuzah
Faithful Guard

A *mezuzah* is a small scroll of parchment with Hebrew text handwritten by a *sofer*, a specially trained scribe (who can also write *Torah* scrolls). Inside are the first two portions of *Shema* that command us to have *mezuzot*. The scroll is rolled up and secured firmly to the doorpost. Even though it is nice for a *mezuzah* to have a beautiful case, it is more important that the parchment inside be made of the best quality material. A *mezuzah* that is written or printed on paper is not valid.

It is a *mitzvah* to put *mezuzot* on the doorposts of every room in our homes and places of business, including basements and garages. (A bathroom or small closet doesn't need a *mezuzah*.) A Jewish home with a *mezuzah* is a holy place, and those who live in it are protected by *Hashem*'s blessings wherever they go.

We place our right hands on a *mezuzah* to kiss it when entering or exiting a doorway. The *mezuzah* reminds us that Hashem is always protecting us.

Where it goes

There are special guidelines for this *mitzvah*. A *mezuzah* must be placed:

- On the right doorpost
- At the bottom of the top third of the doorpost
- In a slanted position—with the top of the *mezuzah* slanted toward the inside of the room
- Right side up (not upside down)

Placing *mezuzot* correctly can be complex, so call your rabbi for help.

How to bless

Before attaching a *mezuzah* to a doorpost, say
this *brachah* (blessing):

בָּרוּךְ אַתָּה יְיָ, אֱלֹהֵינוּ מֶלֶךְ הָעוֹלָם, אֲשֶׁר
קִדְּשָׁנוּ בְּמִצְוֹתָיו, וְצִוָּנוּ לִקְבּוֹעַ מְזוּזָה:

**Ba-ruch Atah A-donai, Elo-haynu Melech
ha-olam, asher kid'sha-nu b'mitz-votav,
v'tzi-vanu likbo-a mezuzah.**

WHAT DOES IT MEAN?

*Blessed are You, L-rd, our G-d, King of the universe,
Who made us holy with His commandments and
commanded us to affix a mezuzah.*

Check it out

Temperature and weather changes, as well as age, may cause
the ink of a *mezuzah's* scroll to fade or crack, making it unfit
for use. *Mezuzot* must be checked by a reliable scribe at least
twice every seven years. Some people have their *mezuzot*
checked once a year. The best time to do so is in the
month of *Elul*, before the new year begins.

TRY IT!

Take a tour around your
house. See how many
mezuzot you need and
where they belong.

Tefillin
Straps to Wrap

What?

Tefillin are two specially-designed boxes worn both on the arm (called *tefillin shel yad*) and on the head (called *tefillin shel rosh*). The outer part of the *tefillin* is made of perfectly square black leather boxes. Inside the boxes are handwritten parchment scrolls, called *parshiyot,* which contain passages from the *Torah* where the commandment of *tefillin* is mentioned, including the *Shema*.

Who?

Tefillin are worn by Jewish men and boys over the age of 13.

When?

Tefillin are worn every weekday during morning prayers. They may be worn any time of the day until sunset and are not worn on *Shabbat*, holidays, or at night.

How?

The *tefillin* s*hel yad* are worn on a person's weaker arm. This means that righties wear the *tefillin* on their left arms and lefties wear the *tefillin* on their right arms. The *tefillin* s*hel yad* are put on first, on the upper part of the arm.

Make a blessing

Before putting on the *tefillin shel yad*, we say this blessing:

בָּרוּךְ אַתָּה יְיָ, אֱלֹהֵינוּ מֶלֶךְ הָעוֹלָם,
אֲשֶׁר קִדְּשָׁנוּ בְּמִצְוֹתָיו,
וְצִוָּנוּ לְהָנִיחַ תְּפִלִּין:

**Ba-ruch Atah A-donai, Elo-haynu Melech
ha-olam, asher kid'sha-nu b'mitz-votav,
v'tzi-vanu l'hani-ach tefillin.**

WHAT DOES IT MEAN?

*Blessed are You, L-rd, our G-d, King of the universe,
who made us holy with His commandments, and
commanded us to put on tefillin.*

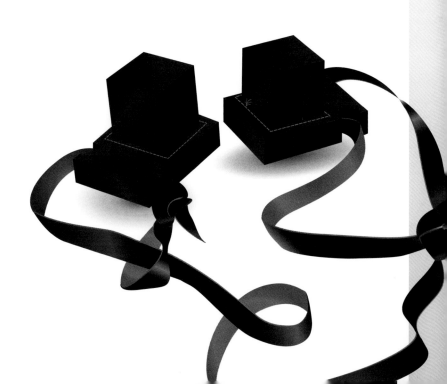

Next, the *tefillin shel rosh* are placed just above the hairline and centered between the eyes. If the person wearing them spoke in between putting on the *tefillin shel yad* and *tefillin shel rosh*, he also says a second blessing:

בָּרוּךְ אַתָּה יְיָ, אֱלֹהֵינוּ מֶלֶךְ הָעוֹלָם,
אֲשֶׁר קִדְּשָׁנוּ בְּמִצְוֹתָיו,
וְצִוָּנוּ עַל מִצְוַת תְּפִלִּין:

Ba-ruch Atah A-donai, Elo-haynu Melech ha-olam, asher kid'sha-nu b'mitz-votav, v'tzi-vanu al mitzvat tefillin.

WHAT DOES IT MEAN?

Blessed are You, L-rd, our G-d, King of the universe, who made us holy with His commandments, and commanded us concerning the mitzvah of tefillin.

Like *mezuzot*, *tefillin* scrolls need to be checked regularly by a qualified scribe.

A Jewish Uniform
Hashem's Soldiers

Like all soldiers, Jewish boys and girls have special uniforms that they wear with pride.

Up top

The uniform for a boy is a *kipah* and *tzitzit*. A *kipah* is a head covering worn as a reminder that *Hashem* is above, always watching everything that we say and do. A Jewish boy wears a *kipah* or other head-covering when he says prayers or blessings. A soldier in Tzivos Hashem (G-d's Army) keeps his head covered all the time—whether he is playing, sleeping, eating, or learning *Torah*.

> *Kipah* and *tzitzit* are not worn in the shower or in the pool.

Married men, and some boys over the age of *Bar Mitzvah*, have the custom to wear a *tallit gadol* (large prayer shawl) during morning prayers.

On the fringe

Tzitzit are the specially knotted threads of wool that are tied onto the corners of a garment. Only clothes that have four corners need *tzitzit*. Since most clothes today do not have four corners, Jewish men and boys wear a four-cornered garment beneath their clothing with *tzitzit* attached so that they can keep this *mitzvah*. This garment is called a *tallit katan* (small prayer shawl).

Every morning before *tzitzit* are put on, the strings need to be checked. If the strings are torn, the *tzitzit* must be fixed and cannot be worn (except in some cases). Ask your rabbi for more information.

To make the blessing, all strings from each corner are taken into the right hand (or left hand, for lefties) and the following is said:

בָּרוּךְ אַתָּה יְיָ, אֱלֹהֵינוּ מֶלֶךְ
הָעוֹלָם, אֲשֶׁר קִדְּשָׁנוּ בְּמִצְוֹתָיו,
וְצִוָּנוּ עַל מִצְוַת צִיצִית:

**Ba-ruch Atah A-donai,
Elo-haynu Melech ha-olam,
asher kid'sha-nu b'mitz-votav,
v'tzi-vanu al mitzvat tzitzit.**

WHAT DOES IT MEAN?

Blessed are You, L-rd, our G-d, King of the world, who made us holy with His commandments, and commanded us concerning the mitzvah of fringes.

Boys wear *tzitzit* to remind them of the 613 *mitzvot*. How so?

צִיצִית=600
The Hebrew letters of the word "tzitzit" have the value of 600.

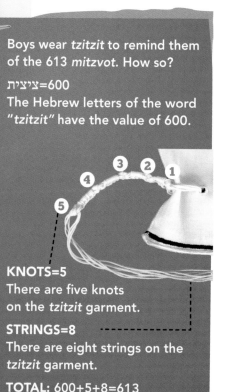

KNOTS=5
There are five knots on the *tzitzit* garment.

STRINGS=8
There are eight strings on the *tzitzit* garment.

TOTAL: 600+5+8=613

Let's be modest

The uniform for Jewish girls requires that they dress according to the guidelines of *tzniut* (modesty). Tz*niut* is one of the essential qualities of the Jewish people. Even when the Jews lived among the Egyptians and Canaanites, who were some of the most immodest nations in the whole world, they remained modest and did not behave like them.

The *Torah* says about Jewish women and girls, *"Happy is their lot and great is their merit,"* because they observe this important commandment. One aspect of *tzniut* for girls and women is dressing modestly: wearing skirts that cover the knees, sleeves that cover the elbows, and necklines that cover the collarbone.

Tzniut also applies to boys and men, because it defines the way we hold ourselves. Modest speech means talking at an appropriate volume and using gentle words. *Tzniut* also means doing good deeds discreetly and not showing off our accomplishments or possessions. *Hashem* loves to see His children acting modestly.

My Tzivot Hashem Room
A Mini-Temple

In the *Beit Hamikdash* (Holy Temple) in Jerusalem, *Hashem's* presence dwelled for many years. Without the *Beit Hamikdash*, you can make your home into a dwelling place for *Hashem* by including three important items in your room, which correspond to some of the holy vessels in the *Beit Hamikdash*.

 = A *Chumash*, where the first five books of the *Torah* are written, represents the Holy Ark of the *Beit Hamikdash*

 = A *Siddur* represents the Altar, because our prayers are like sacrifices

 = A *tzedakah* box represents the *Shulchan* (Table), where the showbread was kept in the *Beit Hamikdash*

In your *Chumash*, *Siddur*, and on your *tzedakah* box, be sure to write the Hebrew words "לַה' הָאָרֶץ וּמְלוֹאָהּ"—The earth and everything inside of it belongs to Hashem." Underneath, sign your Jewish name to affirm that you believe these words are true.

Every day, make sure to set aside some time to learn *Torah* from your *Chumash*, pray with your *Siddur*, and put a coin in the *tzedakah* box. Attaching a *tzedakah* box to the wall makes your room holy, and it will also remind you to give daily.

A Letter for Every Kid
Your Army ID

Which is the most important letter in the whole *Torah*? Is there one that the *Torah* can do without?

If a single one of the *Torah's* 304,805 letters is missing, the whole scroll is invalid and cannot be used until it is fixed. So if someone asks, "Which is the most important letter in the *Sefer Torah* (Torah scroll)?" the answer is, "Every single one!"

All armies have registration books listing every soldier. Our letters in the *Torah* are like our "army IDs"—proof that we are soldiers in Tzivos Hashem.

Children from across the globe unite through buying a letter in a *Torah* scroll. The *Torah* tells us that children are considered pure and clear of sin. The children's unity through the *Torah* is especially precious to *Hashem*. Each Jewish child having their own letter in a *Torah* scroll unites all the Jewish people with each other and with our precious *Torah*.

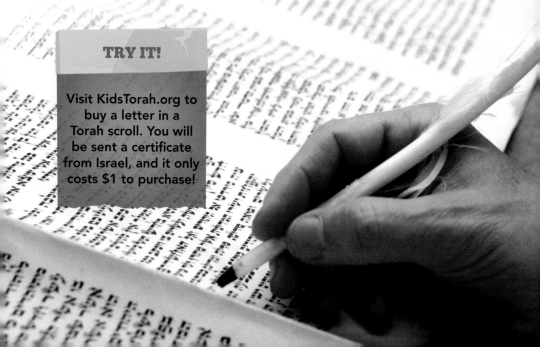

TRY IT!

Visit KidsTorah.org to buy a letter in a Torah scroll. You will be sent a certificate from Israel, and it only costs $1 to purchase!

Mivtzoim
The Mitzvah Campaigns

Help a friend get involved in Judaism! Here are some fundamental *mitzvot* that the Lubavitcher Rebbe emphasized for every Jew to learn about and practice. Are you familiar with them all?

- **Ahavat Yisrael:** Love your fellow Jew as you love yourself

- **Chinuch:** Receive and give a *Torah*-true education

- **Torah:** Study every day and every night

- **Mezuzah:** Affix a *mezuzah* on the right doorpost of every room in your house

- **Tefillin:** Put on *tefillin* every weekday (men and boys 13 years of age and over)

- **Tzedakah:** Give charity every weekday

- **Candle-lighting:** Light candles on the eve of every *Shabbat* and *yom tov* (holiday) at the proper time, reciting the appropriate blessings (all women, starting from three years old)

- **Kosher:** Observe the kosher dietary laws at home, and wherever else you may be

- **Jewish books:** Supply your home with at least the most fundamental holy books: a *Chumash*, *Siddur* and *Tehillim* (Psalms)

Family purity: For a happy, healthy, and united family, parents observe the *mitzvah* of family purity

A letter in a Sefer Torah: Use your own money to buy a letter in a *Sefer Torah*

Rambam: Study Maimonides' *Book of Mitzvot*

Jewish Holidays

As each month passes, we commemorate the ups and downs of our history, celebrating the times when we listened to Hashem (G-d), which made us the most powerful nation on earth.

Rosh Chodesh
Schedule of the Moon

The Jewish calendar is different from other calendars. A Jewish month begins when the new moon appears, is halfway through when the moon is fullest, and ends when the moon has gotten so small that it disappears. The cycle of the moon reminds us of our history as a people—although at times we have been so oppressed that it seemed like we would disappear, ultimately we always return to our full strength.

In the Jewish calendar there are 354 days a year, 11 days less than a solar calendar year. To make sure that the holiday of *Pesach* (Passover) always falls out in the springtime, a leap year happens approximately every three years. In a leap year, a thirteenth month, a second Adar is added. When that happens, *Purim* and its observances (along with birthdays and anniversaries) are celebrated in the second month of Adar.

Rosh Chodesh, the beginning of a new Jewish month, is a special time to reflect on the past and make good resolutions for the future.

TRY IT!

Get a Jewish calendar of your own, or fill in the Jewish holidays on a regular calendar.

Yomim Tovim
Holiday Spirit

A *yom tov* (Jewish holiday) is observed in a manner similar to *Shabbat*. We celebrate by doing special *mitzvot* (commandments), eating special foods, and saying special prayers. We light candles before sunset and say a *brachah* (blessing). On *Yom Tov* we say a special *Kiddush* and make *Havdalah*. As on *Shabbat*, we don't do weekday activities, aside from some types of cooking that are allowed.

Middle days

The holidays of *Sukkot* and *Pesach* (Passover) have unique schedules. The first and last two days of *Sukkot* and *Pesach* are *yomim tovim* (holidays), when we light candles before sundown and do not work. The days in between are referred to as *Chol Hamoed,* or middle days, when we may use electricity and perform some types of necessary work, like driving.

Can you memorize the candle-lighting *brachah* for *yomim tovim* (holidays)? Find the text in a *Siddur*.

The Jewish months

See if you can learn the names, along with any holidays that occur during each month.

- *Tishrei*
- *Cheshvan*
- *Kislev*
- *Tevet*
- *Shvat*
- *Adar*

- *Nissan*
- *Iyar*
- *Sivan*
- *Tammuz*
- *Av*
- *Elul*

TISHREI

1

TISHREI

Rosh Hashanah
Head of the Year

Tishrei

1-2

Rosh Hashanah is the Jewish New Year, when we accept *Hashem* (G-d) as our king. On this day, *Hashem* completed creation. *Rosh Hashanah* is the day of judgment for the entire world, when *Hashem* decides who will be inscribed in the Book of Life for the year to come. It is a time for making good resolutions for the new year ahead, like deciding to learn *Torah* more often and do more *mitzvot*.

HOW TO CELEBRATE

Wake-up call

The sound of the *shofar* (ram's horn) awakens us to return to *Hashem*. This returning is called *teshuvah*. The *shofar's* blast is like a cry of regret over past misdeeds and a longing to come closer to *Hashem*. The sound also proclaims *Hashem* as King of the world, just as trumpets are used to crown a human king.

DID YOU KNOW?
The coming of *Mashiach* (the Messiah) will also be announced with the blast of a *shofar*.

Signs of the times

We celebrate *Rosh Hashanah* with a festive meal, feeling confident that *Hashem* has accepted our prayers. At the *Rosh Hashanah* feast, we eat symbolic foods: the head of a fish, to be like a head and not like a tail; round *challahs*, so that our blessings will be complete; and pomegranates, so that our year will be packed with *mitzvot* the way a pomegranate is full of seeds. Since we want to merit a sweet new year, we also eat apples dipped in honey and other sweet dishes, like sweetened carrots. On the second night, we have new fruits on which to say the *brachah* of *Shehecheyanu*.

TRY IT!

For the full brachah of shehecheyanu, refer to section 2, page 43.

Tashlich

On the first afternoon of *Rosh Hashanah*, we go to a pond or river where fish swim and say a prayer called *Tashlich*. We "throw" our sins into the water and beg *Hashem* for mercy. The fish, with their open eyes, remind us that *Hashem* is always looking out for us. If the first day of *Rosh Hashanah* is on *Shabbat*, we perform the *tashlich* service on the second day.

Aseres Yemei Teshuva
Ten Days of Repentance

Tishrei

1-10

Opportune Time

There are ten days from *Rosh Hashanah* until *Yom Kippur*, called the Ten Days of Repentance. While the judgment of an upcoming year is written on *Rosh Hashanah*, it is only on *Yom Kippur* that the verdict is sealed. Therefore, the days in between are a very serious time, during which we try our hardest to perfect our behavior so that our decrees will be changed for the better. We say extra prayers, give more *tzedakah* (charity) than usual, and are very careful with what we say and do. This is also a good time to ask for forgiveness from anyone whose feelings we may have hurt during the year. When *Hashem* sees us forgiving those around us, He forgives us for our sins as well.

Tzom Gedaliah
Fast of Gedaliah

Tishrei

3

A day of fasting

The day after *Rosh Hashanah* is a fast day, commemorating the assassination of Gedaliah, son of Achikam. He was killed a few years after the destruction of the second *Beit Hamikdash* (Holy Temple) in the year 422 BCE. After the Land of Israel was conquered by the Babylonians, the Jews were allowed to remain under a Jewish governor's rule. Gedaliah was a righteous leader and a member of King David's royal family. His death was a great tragedy, setting into motion the exile from the Land of Israel for all remaining Jews.

On this day, as on all fast days, we give extra *tzedakah* and say special prayers.

DID YOU KNOW?
If the day after *Rosh Hashanah* is *Shabbat*, the fast is observed on Sunday instead.

Yom Kippur
Day of Atonement

Tishrei

10

Yom Kippur is the most solemn of all holidays. It is on this day that the entire world's fate for the upcoming year is sealed. Yom Kippur is the last of the Ten Days of Repentance, and it is a time of fasting and prayer. We cleanse ourselves from all of our sins by praying that Hashem will forgive us, so that we can start the new year with clean slates. Yom Kippur is a full-day fast, beginning at sundown and ending at nightfall the following day, the tenth of Tishrei.

HOW TO CELEBRATE

Kapparot

Early in the morning, on the day before Yom Kippur, we perform a ceremony called kapparot. In this customary ritual, we say a prayer while gently waving a live chicken, fish, or money over our heads. The money or animals are donated to charity, and we ask Hashem that we be forgiven in the merit of tzedakah.

Mitzvah meals

Since we need strength to fast, it is a mitzvah to eat two big meals on the day before Yom Kippur. Some have a custom to eat kreplach, a kind of dumpling filled with meat, to symbolize that just as the meat is covered by dough, Hashem's mercy will cover any harsh judgment.

Mikvah

It is customary for some to cleanse in a *mikvah* (ritual bath) before *Yom Kippur*.

Blessing

It is customary for a father to bless his children before *Yom Kippur*.

Fasting

All men and women over the ages of *Bar* and *Bat Mitzvah* (13 years old for boys and 12 for girls) do not eat or drink. Younger children avoid eating for pleasure and can ask their parents to fast a little bit. On *Yom Kippur* we may not wash ourselves, smear ointments, or wear leather shoes.

Prayer

We spend the day in *shul* (synagogue), asking *Hashem* to forgive our sins. We search for ways to improve ourselves. There is also a custom for married men to wear white clothes on *Yom Kippur*, to resemble angels, who are free of sin.

Happy ending

On *Yom Kippur* we say an extra concluding prayer called *Ne'ilah*. As the holiest day of the year comes to a close, we are locked into a private moment with *Hashem*. We proclaim *Shema*, hear the *shofar's* blast, and wish each other "Next year in Jerusalem!" We rejoice, certain that *Hashem* has forgiven our sins and will grant us a good year.

Sukkot
Our Happy Time

Tishrei

15-21

In the hut

During the week-long holiday of *Sukkot*, it is a *mitzvah* to spend time in a hut, called a *sukkah*. The *sukkah* affirms our faith in G-d, reminding us of the miraculous clouds of glory that kept us safe while we traveled through the desert to Israel. The clouds protected the Jews from snakes and scorpions, smoothed the ground, and even cleaned clothing.

The whole me

Spending time in the *sukkah* is a unique *mitzvah*. All other *mitzvot* require us to use only one or some of our limbs, such as our hands or mouths (like when we give charity or pray), but the *mitzvah* of *sukkah* surrounds us from head to toe.

Extra blessing

When eating in the *sukkah* we say an extra *brachah* right after the *brachah* over bread, wine, or *mezonot* foods (see section 2):

- -

בָּרוּךְ אַתָּה יְיָ, אֱלֹהֵינוּ מֶלֶךְ הָעוֹלָם אֲשֶׁר
קִדְּשָׁנוּ בְּמִצְוֹתָיו וְצִוָּנוּ לֵישֵׁב בַּסֻּכָּה:

**Baruch Atah A-donai, Elo-haynu Melech
ha-olam, asher kid'sha-nu b'mitz-votav,
v'tzi-vanu lay-shayv ba-Sukkah.**

WHAT DOES IT MEAN?

*Blessed are You, L-rd, our G-d, King of the universe,
who made us holy with His commandments, and
commanded us to dwell in the sukkah.*

Lulav and etrog

The *mitzvah* of the Four Kinds is observed on *Sukkot*.
We gather four types of plants together:

 Etrog: a citron fruit

 Lulav: a date-palm branch

 Hadasim: three or more branches of myrtle

 Aravot: two willow twigs with their leaves

The Four Kinds represent four types of Jews: the *etrog*
has both smell and taste, like a Jew who learns *Torah* and
does *mitzvot*; the *lulav* comes from a tree with sweet fruit,
but has no smell, like someone whose main occupation is
studying *Torah*; the *hadasim* don't have taste, but give off
a nice aroma, a symbol of those who do good deeds but
don't learn much; the *aravot* have neither taste nor smell,
compared to Jews who do not learn or practice.

The *mitzvah* of bringing them all together shows that we are
incomplete without every Jew. Despite our differences, we
remain a proud, united nation.

On each of the seven days of *Sukkot* (besides *Shabbat*), we
hold the *lulav* bundled with the *hadasim* and *aravot* in our
right hand and the *etrog* in our left (lefties hold the *lulav* in
their left hands).

We say the following blessing over the Four Kinds:

בָּרוּךְ אַתָּה יְיָ, אֱלֹהֵינוּ מֶלֶךְ הָעוֹלָם
אֲשֶׁר קִדְּשָׁנוּ בְּמִצְוֹתָיו וְצִוָּנוּ
עַל נְטִילַת לוּלָב:

Baruch Atah A-donai, Elo-haynu Melech ha-olam, asher kid'sha-nu b'mitz-votav, v'tzi-vanu al n'tilat lulav.

WHAT DOES IT MEAN?

Blessed are You, L-rd, our G-d, King of the universe, who made us holy with His commandments, and commanded us concerning the taking of the lulav.

Give the Four Kinds three gentle shakes in all six directions, symbolizing how Hashem is found everywhere. Before doing the *mitzvah* for the first time this holiday season, add the *Shehechiyanu* blessing (page 43).

Hoshanah Rabbah

On *Hoshanah Rabbah*, the last day of *Sukkot*, the judgment of *Yom Kippur* becomes final. It is customary for men to stay awake on this night and recite words of *Torah* and Psalms. During the day, holding our *lulav* and *etrog*, we circle the *bimah* (synagogue podium) seven times and recite special prayers, asking *Hashem* to bless the year with abundant sustenance.

Shemini Atzeret
A Bonus Day

Tishrei

22

After seven days of *Sukkot*, *Hashem* wants us to keep the celebrations going. We rejoice with the *Torah* on the holiday of *Shemini Atzeret*. Many *shuls* (synagogues) have the custom of taking the *Torah* scrolls out of the Ark and dancing with them, to show our love for learning Torah. This is called *hakafot*. Many people still eat in the *sukkah* on *Shemini Atzeret* (but without reciting the extra *brachah* for eating inside it).

Simchat Torah
Rejoicing with the Torah

Tishrei

23

The day after *Shemini Atzeret* is called *Simchat Torah*. *Simchat Torah* is another day of tremendous joy that energizes us with happiness for the whole year. We take the *Torah* scrolls out of the Ark and dance with them until late at night.

On *Simchat Torah*, we do not eat in the *sukkah* at all.

During the day, we dance with the scrolls again. Then we complete the yearly cycle of *Torah*-reading and start again from the beginning. This is the only time of the year when even little boys are called up to the *Torah*.

TRY IT!

Boys, go to synagogue with your fathers so you, too, can be called up to the Torah!

CHESHVAN

This month has no Jewish holidays, which is why it is sometimes called *Mar-Cheshvan*. (*"Mar"* means "bitter.")

KISLEV

Chanukah
Festival of Lights

Kislev

25

Greek rulers

During the time of the second *Beit Hamikdash*, Syrian-Greek conquerors prohibited the study of *Torah*, forced the Jewish people to worship idols, and defiled the *Beit Hamikdash*.

Fighting back

Mattityahu (Mattathias), a loyal Jew who lived in the town of *Modi'in*, refused to let the persecution continue. Along with his five sons, he gathered a small, brave army of men called the *Maccabees*. This Jewish army was led by Mattityahu's son Yehudah (Judah). Together, they began a rebellion against the vastly superior Syrian-Greek army. Through many miracles, these few Jews won the war and defeated the mighty Syrian-Greeks!

The miracle of the oil

When the *Maccabees* returned to the *Beit Hamikdash*, they wanted to light its *menorah* with the pure olive oil sealed by the *kohen gadol*. But the *Beit Hamikdash* had been looted and desecrated by the Syrian–Greeks, and the only sealed jug they could find contained only enough oil to last for one day's lighting. *Hashem* performed another miracle and made the little jug of oil last for eight days and nights, until fresh oil could be obtained.

Keep the flame alive

To commemorate the miracle of the oil, we light a *menorah* of our own on each night of *Chanukah*. We start with one candle on the first night and add another every night. This way, every night we increase the light we bring to the world. By the eighth night of *Chanukah*, we light eight flames.

Light up the night

Place candles from right to left, then light the candles from left to right using the *shamash*, a candle that is placed apart from the others.

The *Chanukah* candles are lit after sunset and need to burn for at least a half-hour after nightfall. They remind us of *Chanukah*'s miracle, and their light is not to be used for any other purpose.

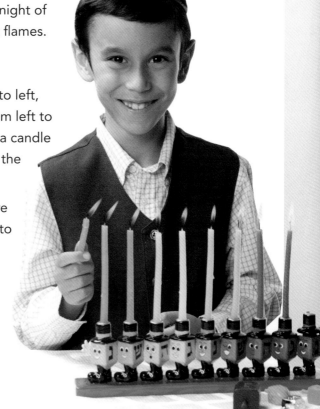

Say these blessings before lighting on every night of *Chanukah*:

בָּרוּךְ אַתָּה יְיָ אֱלֹקֵינוּ מֶלֶךְ הָעוֹלָם
אֲשֶׁר קִדְּשָׁנוּ בְּמִצְוֹתָיו וְצִוָּנוּ
לְהַדְלִיק נֵר חֲנוּכָּה

**Baruch Atah A-donai, Elo-haynu Melech
ha-olam, asher kid'sha-nu b'mitz-votav,
v'tzi-vanu l'hadlik nayr Chanukah.**

WHAT DOES IT MEAN?

*Blessed are You, L-rd, our G-d, King of the universe,
who made us holy with His commandments, and
commanded us to kindle the Chanukah light.*

בָּרוּךְ אַתָּה יְיָ אֱלֹקֵינוּ מֶלֶךְ הָעוֹלָם
שֶׁעָשָׂה נִסִּים לַאֲבוֹתֵינוּ
בַּיָּמִים הָהֵם בַּזְּמַן הַזֶּה

**Baruch Atah A-donai, Elo-haynu Melech
ha-olam, she-asah nisim la-avotaynu
ba-yamim ha-haym biz-man ha-zeh.**

On the first night
of *Chanukah*,
add the
Shehechiyanu
blessing (see
page 43).

WHAT DOES IT MEAN?

*Blessed are You, L-rd, our G-d, King of the
universe, who performed miracles for our
forefathers in those days, at this time.*

Spin it

An ancient game that never gets old—everyone loves playing *dreidel*! When Greeks banned *Torah* study, brave Jewish children hid in caves to learn. When soldiers came around to enforce the decrees, they quickly put away their books and got busy with these innocent spinning tops. The four letters on the *dreidel's* sides, *Nun*, *Gimmel*, *Hay*, and *Shin*, stand for Hebrew words that mean "a great miracle happened there."

To play the game, each player starts off with an equal number of coins or candies. To begin, everyone puts one in the center pot. Players take turns spinning *dreidels*. The letter you land on could make it your lucky day!

נ = Do nothing

ג = You get the whole pot!

ה = Take half of what is in the middle

ש = Add one piece to the center

We add the *V'al Hanissim* prayer in the *Amidah* and in the *Birkat Hamazon* (Grace After Meals) to thank *Hashem* for the miracles of *Chanukah*. You can find this extra prayer in a *Siddur*.

TRY IT!

We remember the miracle of oil on *Chanukah* by frying up tasty holiday treats. Try your hand at making traditional *sufganiyot* (jelly doughnuts) or *latkes* (potato pancakes).

TEVET

Asara B'Tevet
The Tenth of Tevet

Tevet

10

On this day over 2,000 years ago, the Babylonian armies surrounded the walls of Jerusalem and laid siege to the city. They prevented all food and water from reaching the city's inhabitants. For two-and-a-half years the Jewish people suffered from hunger. Eventually, on *Tisha B'Av*, the ninth day of *Av*, the Babylonians destroyed the first *Beit Hamikdash*.

To commemorate this tragic event we say special prayers and give extra *tzedakah*. Adults fast from dawn to nightfall.

SHVAT

Chamishah Asar B'Shvat
Fifteenth of Shvat

Shvat
15

Chamishah Asar B'Shvat, also called Tu B'Shvat, is the New Year for Trees. We celebrate by eating different types of fruits, especially those with which the Land of Israel is blessed:

Grapes

Figs

Pomegranates

Dates

Olives

TRY IT!

On *Chamisha Asar B'Shvat*, taste some of these fruits, making the correct blessing before and after.

DID YOU KNOW?
When wheat and barley are added, this list makes up the seven special foods of Israel.

ADAR

Our sages say that when the month of *Adar* begins, we must increase in joy.

Taanit Esther
The Fast of Esther

Adar

13

On the day before *Purim*, we don't eat or drink from dawn until nightfall. We say special prayers and give extra *tzedakah*.

Our fast commemorates the fast that the Jews took upon themselves before they went out to battle their enemies on the 13th day of *Adar*.

Purim
A Day of Joy

Adar

14

Persian exile

Over 2,000 years ago in Persia, the Jewish people were exiled from Israel, eventually coming under the rule of King Achashverosh (Ahasuerus). They prospered financially and socially, but they began to forget *Torah* and *mitzvot*. King Achashverosh appointed a wicked minister named Haman, who hated the Jews and plotted to kill every Jewish man, woman, and child on the 13th day of *Adar*.

Esther saves the day

Meanwhile, Esther, who Achashverosh had chosen to be his queen, was hiding the fact that she was Jewish. When she heard of Haman's plan, she encouraged the Jews to observe three days of fasting and prayer. Mordechai, the leader of the Jewish people, gathered 22,000 children and taught them *Torah*. The Jews wholeheartedly returned to *Hashem*.

Then Esther went to Achashverosh and revealed her identity as a Jew. She asked that the king spare the lives of her people. The king was furious with Haman and ordered that he be killed on the gallows built for Mordechai. The tables had been turned!

The Jews were also given permission to defend themselves against their enemies. Every year we celebrate the Purim miracle, a situation that completely turned around.

HOW TO CELEBRATE

Cookies

We eat *hamentash* cookies because the covered filling reminds us of the miracles that were "hidden."

Costumes

On *Purim* it is customary for children to dress up in costumes, symbolizing the miracles *Hashem* "dressed up" to seem natural.

TRY IT!

Dress up as a Jewish hero this *Purim*!

Prayer

We add the prayer *V'Al Hanissim* in the *Amidah* and in *Birkat Hamazon* to thank *Hashem* for the miracles of *Purim*. You can find this extra prayer in a *Siddur*.

Charity

During the time that the *Beit Hamikdash* was standing, each person would give a half *shekel* (a currency used at the time) to contribute to the communal sacrifices. We commemorate this *mitzvah* today by giving the equivalent of three half-*shekel* coins to *tzedakah*. In America, for example, that means giving three silver half-dollars.

Join the party

There are four *mitzvot* of *Purim*:

- *Megillah*: On *Purim* night and day we read a scroll that relates the story of *Purim*. When Haman's name is mentioned, we twirl noisemakers, called *graggers,* and stamp our feet to "drown out" his evil name.

- *Mishloach Manot*: We send a gift with at least two kinds of ready-to-eat foods to at least one friend.

- *Matanot L'evyonim*: We spread *Purim* joy by giving *tzedakah* to at least two poor people.

- *Mishteh*: We rejoice with a special *Purim* meal.

Shushan Purim
Purim, Take Two

Adar

15

King Achashverosh granted the Jews of Persia one day—the 13th of *Adar*—to fight against their enemies. Shushan, the capital city, was given an extra day for war. On the fourteenth of *Adar*, when all Jews from outlying regions were celebrating their victory, the Jews of Shushan were still waging battle and did not celebrate until the next day, the fifteenth. Because Shushan was completely surrounded by walls, cities today that have had walls since the time of Yehoshua (Joshua), such as Jerusalem, commemorate the extra day by celebrating *Purim* on the 15th of *Adar*.

NISSAN

Pesach
Passover

Nissan
15-22

Over 3,000 years ago we were slaves to Pharaoh in Egypt. On *Pesach*, *Hashem* took us out with great miracles, redeeming us so that we could serve Him.

Pesach offering

Following *Hashem*'s commandment, on the very first *Pesach*, the night before leaving Egypt, the Jews roasted and ate a lamb as a sacrifice called the *korban Pesach*. Later, in the times of the *Beit Hamikdash*, the lamb offering was brought every *Pesach* eve.

Clean up time

Hashem tells us not to eat, own, or even see our *chametz* on *Pesach*. *Chametz* means anything made from the wheat, barley, rye, oats, or spelt that has risen. This includes any flour that touched water and was not fully baked within 18 minutes. Bread, cookies, pasta, and cereal are all examples of *chametz*.

For sale

Any *chametz* not thrown away is locked up, sold to a non-Jew, and bought back after the holiday.

TRY IT!

Your parents can sell *chametz* by visiting **chabad.org/sellchametz**.

Hide and seek

The night before *Pesach*, we search for *chametz* with a candle, feather, and wooden spoon in a ritual called *Bedikat Chametz*. Traditionally, we hide ten peices of bread around the house beforehand, to be found while searching for *chametz*.

Burning

The following morning we stop eating *chametz* and burn any *chametz* found the night before.

TRY IT!

Find out the exact times for pre-Passover rituals on *chabad.org/passover*.

Passover bread

We eat *matzah*, a bread made of only pure flour and water, on *Pesach*. The dough is kneaded and baked in less than 18 minutes so that it does not have a chance to rise and become *chametz*. At the special *Pesach* meal, called the *Seder*, it is a *mitzvah* to eat *matzah*, which reminds us of the dough that did not have time to rise when the Jews left Egypt in a hurry. Eating *matzah* at the *Seder* strengthens our faith in *Hashem*.

Shmurah Matzah

Shmurah matzah means "guarded *matzah*." It is made with flour that is carefully guarded from the time the wheat is harvested to make sure it doesn't come into contact with water and become *chametz*. *Shmurah matzah*, specifically when it is handmade, is the best kind to use for the *Seder* and throughout the holiday.

Seder

On the first two nights of *Pesach*, we hold a *Seder*. We read from a book called the *Haggadah*. Children ask the Four Questions, starting with "Why is this night different from all others?" The questions are answered with the story of our exodus: had *Hashem* not redeemed us, we would still be enslaved to Pharaoh in Egypt. We eat a festive *yom tov* meal afterward, complete with *matzah* and four cups of wine or grape juice.

Sefirat Ha'Omer
Countdown to the Torah

What?

When the Jewish people left Egypt, they counted in anticipation of receiving the *Torah* on Mount Sinai. Therefore, beginning on the second night of *Pesach*, we count 49 days—exactly seven weeks—from *Pesach* until *Shavuot*. This counting is called *Sefirat Ha'Omer*. Every day we work on a different aspect of our character to refine ourselves in preparation for receiving Hashem's special gift.

How?

Every night we recite a *brachah* and count the *Omer*. For example, on the 15th day of the *Omer*, we say, "Today is 15 days, which is two weeks and one day of the *Omer*."

Special customs

Many years ago, during the *Sefirat HaOmer* period, thousands of Rabbi Akiva's students died from a plague. The weeks from *Pesach* to *Shavuot* are therefore considered a time of mourning. There are no weddings, and we don't listen to music or get haircuts. Since the plague was caused by the students' lack of respect for one another, these weeks are a time to increase in acts of *Ahavat Yisrael*, love for our fellow Jews.

Shevi'i Shel Pesach
Seventh Day of Passover

Nissan

21

After the Jews left Egypt, Pharaoh's army chased after them, trapping them at the shores of the *Yam Suf* (Sea of Reeds). On the seventh day after the exodus, *Hashem* miraculously split the sea and the Jews crossed through to dry land. When the Egyptian army tried to follow the Jews into the sea, walls of water came crashing down, drowning the Egyptians. Then the Jews were truly free. We commemorate this miracle by reading from the *Torah* a song of gratitude that the Jews sang after crossing onto dry land.

Acharon Shel Pesach
Last Day of Passover

Nissan

22

The first days of *Pesach* celebrate the
redemption of the Jews from slavery in Egypt
under the leadership of Moshe (Moses); the last day
celebrates the ultimate redemption from exile under the
leadership of *Mashiach* (the Messiah). Because the last day of
Pesach is so closely connected with *Mashiach*, we read from
the *Torah* about the times of *Mashiach* and hold a special
feast called the *Mashiach seudah* (meal of the Messiah). We
eat *matzah* and drink four cups of wine or grape juice in
anticipation of the redemption.

IYAR

Pesach Sheini
The Second Passover

Iyar

14

On *Pesach* eve, to commemorate the lamb offering the Jews brought in Egypt, every Jew brought a lamb to be sacrificed in the *Beit Hamikdash*. If for some reason they were not able to come on that day, their second chance was on *Pesach Sheini* (the second *Pesach*), exactly one month later. Today, even though we cannot offer this sacrifice in the *Beit Hamikdash*, we celebrate *Pesach Sheini* by eating *matzah*. This reminds us that *Hashem* always gives us a second chance; it's never too late to return.

Lag B'Omer
33rd Day of the Omer

Iyar
18

On this day, the terrible plague that caused the death of Rabbi Akiva's students came to an end. Of the 24,000 who perished, five students survived the epidemic. One of them, Rabbi Shimon bar Yochai (also called Rashbi), was the great sage who wrote the *Zohar*, a mystical book that reveals the *Torah*'s secret teachings. Years later he also passed away on this day.

HOW TO CELEBRATE

Rabbi Shimon bar Yochai asked that the date of his death be commemorated as a day of joy. Children celebrate *Lag B'Omer* by participating in bonfires, visiting parks, and playing with toy bows and arrows. In many places, *Lag B'Omer* is celebrated with a special parade demonstrating Jewish pride and unity. It is a custom for boys who turn three years old between the first day of *Pesach* and *Lag B'Omer* to have their first haircut on this occasion.

DID YOU KNOW?
"*Lag*" is a nickname for "33," referring to its day in the *Omer* count.

We play with bows and arrows since they share the same letters as the Hebrew word for "rainbow." During Rashbi's lifetime, Hashem never showed a rainbow (a sign of His displeasure).

SIVAN

Shavuot
Giving of the Torah

Sivan
6-7

Shavuot commemorates the day we received the Torah from Hashem. When Hashem offered the Torah to the Jews at Mount Sinai, they immediately said, "Na'aseh v'nishmah" which means, "We will do and we will listen." Before the Jewish people knew what was written in the Torah, they accepted it wholeheartedly. Every Shavuot, we renew our dedication to Hashem's gift.

HOW TO CELEBRATE

On the first night of *Shavuot*, men stay up all night learning *Torah*. In the morning we go to *shul* and hear the Ten Commandments read aloud from a *Sefer Torah* (*Torah* scroll). Just like we were all present at the original giving of the *Torah*, it is very important for everyone to attend the *Shavuot* reading: men, women, children, and even little babies.

Why?

Before *Hashem* gave us the *Torah*, He wanted a guarantee that we would always keep its laws. The rabbis gave their guarantee, but *Hashem* wouldn't accept it. Next the teachers tried, then the prophets, grandparents, and parents. *Hashem* did not agree to give the *Torah* until the children were offered as guarantors. Only then did *Hashem* promise to make us His chosen nation.

The *Torah* was only given because of the children who committed to uphold it. You are the guarantors for all the Jewish people! It is up to you to keep the *Torah* alive today.

Cheesecake time

Because the *Torah* is compared to milk, we eat dairy products to celebrate. The *Shavuot* day menu might include blintzes, cheesecake, or ice cream. We then wait one hour before eating a traditional holiday meal with meat.

TAMMUZ

Shiva Asar B'Tammuz
17th of Tammuz

Tammuz

17

We fast on this day for the following reasons:

- *Moshe* brought down the *Luchot* (the tablets on which the Ten Commandments were written) from Mount Sinai, and he saw that the Jews were worshipping the Golden Calf. He broke the holy tablets in response.

- The Romans knocked down Jerusalem's walls, allowing them to destroy the second *Beit Hamikdash* three weeks later.

The Three Weeks
Mourning Time

Tammuz-Av

17-9

The Three Weeks are a time when, throughout history, many tragedies befell the Jewish people. Terrible decrees were enacted and a great number of Jews were killed. During this period, we recall the terrible tragedies that the Jewish people suffered and prepare for the redemption.

Sad for the past, hopeful for the future

As a sign of mourning, during this time we do not:

- Cut hair
- Celebrate weddings
- Listen to music

During this time we:

- Give extra *tzedakah*
- Increase in acts of kindness
- Learn about the *Beit Hamikdash* and *Mashiach*

AV

Tisha B'Av
Ninth of Av

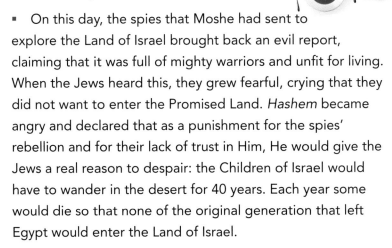

The day of *Tisha B'Av* recalls many tragic events that happened throughout Jewish history:

- On this day, the spies that Moshe had sent to explore the Land of Israel brought back an evil report, claiming that it was full of mighty warriors and unfit for living. When the Jews heard this, they grew fearful, crying that they did not want to enter the Promised Land. *Hashem* became angry and declared that as a punishment for the spies' rebellion and for their lack of trust in Him, He would give the Jews a real reason to despair: the Children of Israel would have to wander in the desert for 40 years. Each year some would die so that none of the original generation that left Egypt would enter the Land of Israel.

- The first *Beit Hamikdash* was destroyed by the Babylonians, and nearly 500 years later, the second Temple was destroyed by the Romans.

Although the ninth of *Av* is the saddest day in the Jewish calendar, it will become the greatest *yom tov* when *Mashiach* comes. May it be so this year!

- Years after the second destruction, the mighty fortress in Beitar, Israel, the stronghold of the Jews' revolution against the Romans, fell in battle.

- In the year 1492, the Jews were expelled from Spain in the infamous Spanish Inquisition.

HOW TO OBSERVE

Tisha B'Av is a full-day fast, starting from sundown and ending with nightfall the following day. Older children try to fast for at least part of the day and younger children do not eat for pleasure. We give extra *tzedakah* and say special prayers. In *shul* we mourn the destruction of the *Beit Hamikdash* by reading the book of *Eichah* (Lamentations) and reciting a text called *Kinot* (Elegies). As a sign of mourning, we do not sit on chairs until noon. We do not bathe or take showers, wear leather shoes, or apply lotions.

Tu B'Av
Fifteenth of Av

The 15th of *Av* marks the end of *Hashem*'s decree that the Jews must wander in the wilderness for 40 years. On this day, the men who were punished for listening to the spies stopped dying, and the Jewish people were at last able to enter the Holy Land.

This day is a joyous holiday. It is said that in the days of the *Beit Hamikdash*, there were no happier days in Israel than *Tu B'Av* and *Yom Kippur*. On this day, the girls of Jerusalem would go out to dance in the vineyards, and everyone rejoiced.

ELUL

The month of *Elul* is a time when we examine our actions of the past year. We decide what we will do to improve ourselves for the upcoming year. During this time, *Hashem* is easy to approach, like a king who goes out into the field where anyone can meet with him. In the month of *Elul*, *Hashem* listens closely to our prayers and forgives us more readily.

It is customary to check our *mezuzot* and *tefillin* in the month of *Elul*.

Every day during the month of *Elul*, we blow the *shofar* to remind us that *Rosh Hashanah*, the day of judgment, is coming soon. This is a good time to wish everyone a happy and healthy new year.

SECTION 6

Jewish Life Cycle

From the moment of birth until a person's final breath, there is a Jewish way to commemorate each stage. Soldiers of Tzivos Hashem mark each milestone with joy, knowing that, as time goes on, we gain more wisdom in how to fulfill our mission on this earth.

BIRTH

A Special Time
Happy Birthday

Every year, the Jewish tradition celebrates the anniversary of our arrival upon this earth. As our birthdays arrive, we are given extra strength to carry out our unique missions in life.

When is it?

Our Jewish birthday usually falls out on a different day than our legal birthday does, because of the Hebrew calendar's unique setup. Ask a parent or teacher to help you look up your Jewish birthday on *chabad.org/birthday*.

How to celebrate

Our birthdays are a time to get together with friends, increase in good deeds, give extra *tzedakah* (charity), and learn more *Torah*. It's also an excellent opportunity for us to make good resolutions for the coming year.

TRY IT!

Ask your rabbi about signing up for Tzivos Hashem's Jewish birthday club!

Your Soul's Identity
All in the Name

Every Jewish child needs a Jewish name, which is often Hebrew or Yiddish. Our Jewish names reflect the essential character of our souls. Do you know who you were named after?

A Jewish boy is given his name at the *brit milah* (circumcision) ceremony; a Jewish girl is given hers at a *Torah* reading after she is born.

Do you know your Jewish name? Write it in the front of this book. If you were never given a Jewish name, ask your parents or rabbi about getting one.

DID YOU KNOW?
Aside from your Jewish name, you also have a Jewish title, based on your family's tribe: *Kohen*, *Levi*, or *Yisrael*.

HELLO
my name is
Yaakov

Brit Milah
It's a Boy

When?

As a Jewish boy turns eight days old, it is a *mitzvah* (commandment) for him to be circumcised. If a person was not circumcised then, the obligation still remains.

Why?

The *mitzvah* of *brit milah* was the first commandment *Hashem* (G-d) gave to our forefather Avraham (Abraham). A *brit milah* is a sign of the everlasting bond *Hashem* has with the Jewish people, making us His special nation.

How?

A circumcision must be performed by a *mohel* (rabbi specially trained in *brit milah*), not by a doctor.

Pidyon Haben
Firstborn Privilege

What?

The *Pidyon Haben* is a special ceremony where a firstborn son is redeemed.

Why?

A son who is a firstborn is called a *bechor*. Originally, all firstborn boys were to serve in the *Beit Hamikdash* (Holy Temple). After the sin of the Golden Calf, *Hashem* took this privilege away from the firstborn sons and gave it to the tribe of *Levi* instead, because they did not participate in the sin. However, a firstborn son still belongs to *Hashem*, and he has to be redeemed or "bought back" through the *Pidyon Haben* ceremony.

Are you a firstborn son? Ask your rabbi about having a *Pidyon Haben* if you have not yet had one!

How?

When a *bechor* is 30 days old, the parents "redeem" the child from a *Kohen* in exchange for five silver coins. The ceremony is celebrated with a festive meal.

The ceremony is held only when the firstborn child is a boy, delivered naturally, and when neither parent is a *Kohen* or *Levi*.

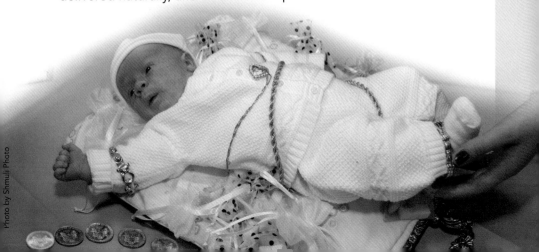

GROWING UP

Upshernish
First Haircut

What?

The Jewish custom is to not cut a boy's hair until he is three years old. When his hair is finally cut, the special occasion is called an *upshernish.* An *upshernish* marks the beginning of the child's formal Jewish education, and it is on this day that a boy starts wearing a *kipah* and *tzitzit.*

How to celebrate

It is a *mitzvah* for males not to shave hair on the sides of their heads, from the forehead until the bottom of the ear. When cutting a boy's hair for the first time (and any time thereafter), the sidelocks, called *peyot,* are left a bit longer.

Little girls also have their own special *mitzvah*! There is a custom for girls to start lighting *Shabbat* candles alongside their mothers as soon as they are old enough to say the blessing. A child is never too young to start bringing goodness to the world!

Bar and Bat Mitzvah
Becoming an Adult

When a boy turns 13 years old, he becomes a *Bar Mitzvah*. When a girl turns 12, she becomes a *Bat Mitzvah*.

All grown up

On this day, boys and girls are considered adults by the *Torah* and are obligated to keep all the *mitzvot*. This means that from this point on, they are held responsible for all of their actions. Once they reach *Bar* or *Bat Mitzvah* age, Jewish boys and girls must be careful to keep all the commandments of the *Torah*, both the dos and the don'ts, just like adults.

How to celebrate

When a boy becomes a *Bar Mitzvah*, he is called to the *Torah* for the first time and starts to put on *tefillin*. From then on, he is counted in a *minyan* (a group of ten men, the minimum for a congregation) and may even lead prayers.

A *Bar* or *Bat Mitzvah* party is usually celebrated with a festive meal shared by family and friends, during which the *Bar* or *Bat Mitzvah* boy or girl makes a speech about a subject in the *Torah*. The *Bar* or *Bat Mitzvah* is an initiation into fulfilling *Hashem*'s *mitzvot* as an adult.

TRY IT!

Are you preparing for your Bar Mitzvah or Bat Mitzvah? Ask your rabbi for help.

ADULTHOOD

Jewish Marriage
Continuing the Chain

Family lies at the center of Jewish life. When a Jewish man and woman get married, they have a Jewish wedding, called a *chatunah*.

United souls

There are three partners in a Jewish marriage: the husband, the wife, and *Hashem*. When *Hashem* enters the marriage as an active third partner, the marriage is blessed. Before a man and a woman get married, they are each like half a person. However, once they get married, their souls unite as one, and *Hashem* blesses them.

Getting ready

The bride and groom prepare for their upcoming marriage by studying the special laws of the holy *mitzvah* of family purity, *taharat hamishpachah*. On their wedding day, the bride and groom fast and pray; all of their sins are forgiven, just like on *Yom Kippur*.

The ceremony

A Jewish wedding ceremony is called a *chuppah*. The *chuppah* is a canopy draped over four poles. It stands under an open sky, reminding us of *Hashem's* promise to Avraham that the Jewish people would be as many as the stars. The *chuppah* ceremony is a very holy and solemn time. *Hashem's* Divine Presence is actually in attendance! Also joining are the deceased ancestors of the bride and groom, who descend from their heavenly abode. Two Jewish witnesses and an officiating rabbi must be present when the bride and groom stand under the *chuppah* for the ceremony. A *minyan* (group of ten men) is also present.

The bride's face is covered with a veil because the Divine Presence shines through her face at this holy time. The veil also shows that the groom values the bride's inner character traits and not just her external beauty. Under the *chuppah* the *ketubah* (marriage contract) is read. The groom places a ring on his bride's finger, symbolizing that she is now bound to him. Seven blessings are recited over a cup of wine. The groom then smashes a cup with his right foot, to remember the destruction of the *Beit Hamikdash* even at such a joyous occasion. Finally, the bride unveils her face and everyone wishes the couple, *"Mazal tov!"*

Celebrate

After the *chuppah*, there is a large feast with much dancing and rejoicing. It is a great *mitzvah* to celebrate with the bride and groom and bring them joy at their wedding.

Making a match

According to the *Torah*, a valid Jewish marriage is one where the bride and groom are both Jewish. A person is considered Jewish when their mother was born a Jew or has converted according to *Torah* law. Marrying a Jewish man or woman ensures that our timeless heritage is passed on to future generations.

SECTION 7

Jewish Concepts

Discover Judaism's unique perspective on all areas of life. Learn how to conquer the battle within and get the world ready for redemption.

Creation
The Seven Days

In the beginning, there was nothing besides for *Hashem* (G-d). *Hashem* created our world in six days and rested on the seventh. In Hebrew, the word "create" literally means to make something out of nothing. When we "create" something, we are actually just taking materials that already exist and reforming them. Only *Hashem* can truly create.

What did Hashem create on each day?

- **Day One:**
  Light

- **Day Two:**
  The heavens

- **Day Three:**
  Oceans, lakes, and rivers; dry land, grass, flowers, and trees

- **Day Four:**
  The sun, moon, planets, and stars

- **Day Five:**
  Fish, insects, and birds

- **Day Six:**
  Animals and the first people, Adam and Chava (Eve)

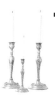
- **Day Seven:**
  Hashem rested on *Shabbat*

DID YOU KNOW?
We rest on *Shabbat* to testify that *Hashem* created the world in six days and rested on the seventh.

Jewish Faith
The Thirteen Principles

 Rambam (Maimonides) was a great *Torah* sage who collected and summarized Jewish law. *Rambam* writes that there are 13 beliefs fundamental to being Jewish.

I believe with complete faith that...

1. *Hashem* is the Creator of the whole world

2. *Hashem* is One

3. *Hashem* has no body or shape

4. *Hashem* is the first and last to ever exist

5. We pray only to *Hashem*

6. All the words of prophets are completely true

7. The prophecy of Moshe (Moses) is eternal, and he is the greatest of all the prophets before and after him

8. The entire *Torah* that we have presently is the same *Torah* that was given to Moshe on Mount Sinai

9. There will never be another *Torah* given from *Hashem*, and His *Torah* will never change

10. *Hashem* knows the deeds and thoughts of every person

11. *Hashem* is just, rewarding those who obey His *mitzvot* (commandments) and punishing those who do not

12. *Mashiach* (the Messiah) will come, and we await his arrival every day

13. There will come a time when *Hashem* will bring the dead back to life

Mashiach
Back to Perfect

A perfect beginning

Over 5,000 years ago, *Hashem* created the first man and woman, Adam and Chava (Eve), in an environment of only goodness: *Gan Eden* (the Garden of Eden).

Adam and *Chava* did not suffer from any pain or illness, and they always had plenty to eat. There was no competition or jealousy; even animals lived in perfect harmony.

Adam and *Chava* had all the time in the world to learn *Torah*. They recognized *Hashem* as the Creator and could speak directly to Him. The world existed as it was meant to be: a place for *Hashem* to call home.

Paradise gone wrong

Adam and Chava sinned by eating from the one tree that
Hashem had forbidden. They were exiled from *Gan Eden* as
a result. Since then, the world has not been the same. The
children of Adam and Chava were tasked with bringing
the world back to its original state of holiness by
learning *Torah* and doing *mitzvot*.

Home again

Since *Hashem* gave us the *Torah* on Mount
Sinai, more than 3,000 years have passed.
During that time men, women, and children have
studied *Torah* and done lots of good deeds, which all add up
to prepare the world for *Mashiach*. That's when our mission
will be complete, with the whole world recognizing *Hashem*
as the Creator and doing only what He wants. Once again the
world will become a place where *Hashem* can feel at home.

Who is Mashiach?

Mashiach is a great, wise, and righteous leader, a true Jewish king who will rebuild the *Beit Hamikdash* and rule over the entire world. *Mashiach* is a descendant of King David. He will teach *Torah* to the entire Jewish people, revealing its secrets like never before. Both the wise and simple, the young and old, will learn from him. He will fight the wars of *Hashem* and strengthen Jewish observance. *Mashiach* will gather all Jews to Israel and help them return to the ways of *Torah* and *mitzvot*.

When Mashiach comes

World peace

There will be justice and harmony worldwide. There will be no famine, war, envy, or competition.

Money and Torah

Good things will be plentiful, and all delights will be as common as the dust of the earth. Because our needs will be taken care of, we will be able to dedicate ourselves solely to learning *Torah* and doing *mitzvot*.

The whole world

All of mankind will seek to know and understand *Hashem*. The entire world will recognize that *Hashem* is the Creator of the world and everyone will serve Him.

A time of miracles

At a later stage of redemption, miracles that defy the laws of nature will occur regularly. Nature as we know it will transform, and what we now consider to be wondrous will become commonplace.

Alive again

One of the Thirteen Principles of Faith is that *Hashem* will revive the dead. At the time of the resurrection, called *techiat hameitim,* every Jew who has ever lived will be brought back to life. We will once again be together with all of our deceased relatives. We will meet Jewish heroes from throughout the ages, including our forefathers Avraham (Abraham), Yitzchak (Isaac), and *Yaakov* (Jacob), as well as Moshe, King David, and Shlomo (Solomon).

Techiat hameitim may take place immediately after *Mashiach* comes, or at some point afterward. However, the great Jewish leaders will arise right away and march with us to greet *Mashiach.*

Heaven on earth

Just as life will change physically, there will also be a radical spiritual shift. We will be able to see *Hashem* in a way that we never have—with our physical eyes.

It's all good

When *Mashiach* comes, with *Hashem's* presence revealed, all those suffering from diseases will be cured. No longer will anyone be blind, deaf, or crippled. Mothers will give birth to babies painlessly. There will no longer be anything to frighten us. Nobody will die anymore; we will all live forever.

Bringing Mashiach: how?

- **Increase in acts of goodness and kindness.** Imagine that the world is balanced on a scale, with one side weighted by goodness and truth and the other by evil and foolishness. If both sides are exactly equal, and we add just a small measure of good, the scale will tip in our favor, bringing *Mashiach* immediately. That small measure could be *your mitzvah*!

- **When you pray, ask *Hashem* to bring *Mashiach*.** In fact, the motto of Tzivos Hashem is "We Want *Mashiach* Now!"

- **Learn about *Mashiach*.** We find out more about what the world will be like in this new era to increase our desire for the ultimate redemption...and to help bring *Mashiach* closer!

The time is now!

We are living in a special time, when technology has transformed the way our world works. Positive change is all around us. As our world becomes more connected, hunger and poverty will soon become a thing of the past. Today's great rabbis have said that we are in the very last moments of exile, and we are standing on the threshold of redemption. If we only open our eyes, we will be able to see that the times of *Mashiach* are not a far-off dream, but something which can be realized here and now!

Which changes in our world show that we are living in the times of *Mashiach*?

Neshamah
The Jewish Soul

Every Jew has a Jewish soul, called a *neshamah*. The *neshamah* inside of us is a part of *Hashem*, which is why we are called the "children of *Hashem*."

Light inside

We can't see or touch our souls, but we can feel them. Our souls give us life. A soul is like a flint stone which always has the potential for fire. Nothing can take away this spark. In the same way, our *neshamah* was created before we were born and lives on forever.

The *Torah* also compares the *neshamah* to a candle. Just as a candle must have oil (or wax) and a wick to keep its flame burning, we need to learn *Torah* and do *mitzvot* to provide the fuel that will keep our souls shining brightly.

Good vs. Evil
The Epic Battle

Do you ever feel like you don't want to do something that you know you really should? Sometimes it feels like there are two "voices" inside of us. One voice encourages us to act nicely and help others, while the other one pushes us to be selfish and do what feels good. We call the good voice the *Yetzer Tov*, or the "good inclination." The other is called the *Yetzer Hara*, the "bad inclination."

Good vs. evil

The *Yetzer Tov* tells us to follow in *Hashem*'s ways: do *mitzvot*, learn *Torah*, be kind to others, and listen to our parents and teachers. The *Yetzer Hara* encourages us to do the opposite of what *Hashem* wants: it tells us to be lazy, selfish, disrespectful, and dishonest. Our job is to ignore the Yetzer Hara and train ourselves to think, speak, and act in a way that makes *Hashem* proud.

It's a trap!

Here's how the *Yetzer Hara* works. First, he tells us to do only a little sin. But when we give in, he gets us to do worse and worse. He can even make doing the wrong thing seem right. How sneaky!

War-zone

Imagine a small city that two kings
are trying to rule over, fighting great
battles in order to conquer it. Our
hearts and minds are like this small city;
the *Yetzer Tov* and *Yetzer Hara* both
want to rule over us. Our job is to make
sure that only the *Yetzer Tov* controls our lives.

Fighting back

The *Yetzer Tov* fights for justice and truth. When we listen to
our holy inner voice, even though it may be very difficult, we
can defeat this enemy inside of us. If we
keep trying, we'll soon have the strength
to listen to the *Yetzer Tov* all the time!
We can win the "battle" over our
hearts and minds when we ignore
the *Yetzer Hara* and keep on doing
what *Hashem* wants.

Eretz Yisrael
The Land of Israel

When *Hashem* created the world, He decided to give the Land of Israel to the Jewish people. No matter where we live, all Jews know that this land is our home. *Hashem* promised our ancestors that their children would inherit the Promised Land. After leaving Egypt, the Jewish people did indeed settle in the land that is ours forever.

Extra goodness

When living in the Land of Israel, we must be extra careful about our behavior, occupying ourselves with *mitzvot* and *Torah*-learning. Many of the *Torah's* 613 *mitzvot* can only be fulfilled in the Land of Israel.

Mashiach times

When *Mashiach* comes, Israel's deserts will be transformed into lush fields and fragrant orchards. Barren thorn bushes will blossom, and trees will grow new fruit every day. *Hashem* will gather all the dispersed Jews from around the world and lead them back to the Promised Land, which will expand its borders so that there will be plenty of room for everyone to live comfortably.

DID YOU KNOW?

The true borders of the Land of Israel, according to the *Torah*, are much wider than the map of Israel is today. It's important for us to remember that Israel is *Hashem's* personal gift to the Jewish People. It will always belong to us, and no person or government has permission to give any parts of it away.

The Beit Hamikdash
A House for Hashem

It is a *mitzvah* to construct a house for *Hashem* in which we can bring offerings and celebrate the three pilgrimage festivals, *Sukkot*, *Pesach* (Passover), and *Shavuot*.

Camping redefined

When the Jews traveled in the desert, *Hashem* commanded them to build a portable sanctuary—the *Mishkan* (Tabernacle)—so that He would be able to dwell among them. The *Mishkan* was not a permanent building: it could be taken apart and moved from place to place. Eventually, King Shlomo (Solomon) built a permanent home for *Hashem*, the *Beit Hamikdash* (Holy Temple) in Jerusalem.

In the courtyard

Offerings in the *Beit Hamikdash* were brought on the great *Mizbe'ach* (Altar), a stone structure which stood in the courtyard. The *Mizbe'ach* was used for burnt offerings (animal and bird sacrifices), meal offerings (made of flour), and the pouring of wine.

Mizbe'ach

Also in the courtyard was the copper *Kiyor*, or wash-basin. The *Kohanim* who participated in the daily offerings washed their hands and feet there before beginning their Temple service.

Kiyor

A holy place

Another section of the *Beit Hamikdash* was called the *Kodesh*, or Holy Chamber. In it were three holy objects made of gold:

- A *Mizbe'ach* for offerings of pleasant-smelling incense
- The *Shulchan* (Table), which held 12 holy loaves of bread
- The *Menorah*, a seven-branched candelabra

Golden Mizbe'ach

The holiest place

The innermost and holiest chamber of the *Beit Hamikdash* was called the *Kodesh Hakadashim*, or "Holy of Holies." It held the *Aron* (Ark), a box of gold-covered wood. The *Aron* contained the two *Luchot* (tablets) engraved with the Ten Commandments, the first set of broken *Luchot*, and the original *Torah* scroll written by *Moshe*.

Shulchan

Aron

Menorah

The Aron journeys

When King Shlomo built the *Beit Hamikdash*, he knew it would ultimately be destroyed. That is why he built secret underground rooms in which to hide the *Aron* together with Aharon's staff, the small vessel of preserved manna, and the oil for anointing *Kohanim*. These items remained hidden during the time of the second *Beit Hamikdash*, and their location will be revealed when the third *Beit Hamikdash* is built, may it be very soon.

Special spot

Today, the site of the *Beit Hamikdash* is called the "Temple Mount" and lies just behind the Western Wall. It is the holiest place in the world. When *Mashiach* comes, the *Beit Hamikdash* will be rebuilt on that site.

DID YOU KNOW?

Shuls (synagogues) around the world are set up so that the congregants pray in the direction of the *Beit Hamikdash*, because all prayers ascend to heaven from there.

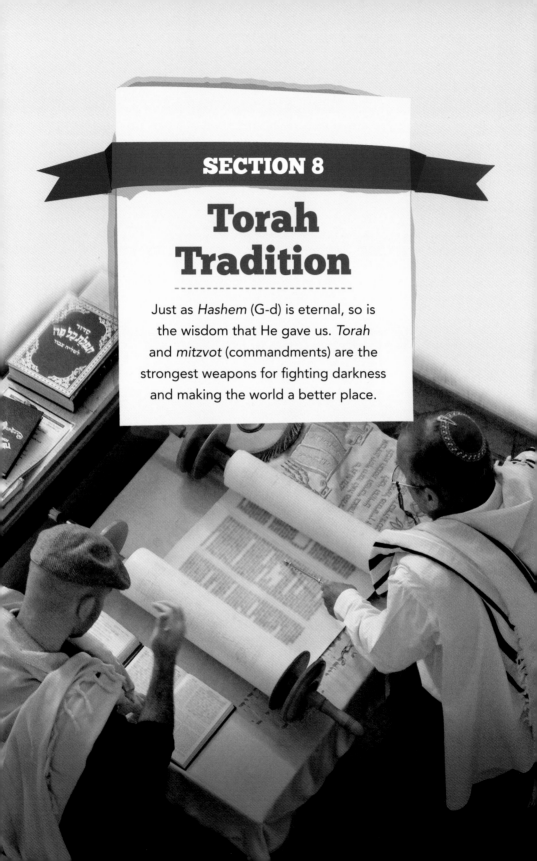

SECTION 8

Torah Tradition

Just as *Hashem* (G-d) is eternal, so is the wisdom that He gave us. *Torah* and *mitzvot* (commandments) are the strongest weapons for fighting darkness and making the world a better place.

Giving of the Torah
Gathered at Sinai

אנכי
לא יהיה
לא תשא
זכור את
כבד את

לא תרצח
לא תנאף
לא תגנב
לא תענה
לא תחמד

Divine Wisdom

Hashem is all powerful: He recreates the entire world at every moment, supervising the lives of every person and animal; guiding vast oceans, continents, planets, stars, and moons. How can we, such small human beings in comparison, stay connected to a force so great?

The question has already been answered for us: before *Hashem* created the world, He put all of His wisdom into the holy *Torah*. By learning its verses, laws, and lessons, we connect to the true essence of the King of all kings!

At Mount Sinai—amid thunder, lightning, and the sounding of the *shofar* (ram's horn)—before the eyes of the entire Jewish people, Moshe received the *Luchot* (Tablets) from *Hashem*. The *Luchot* were two solid, square cubes of sapphire, exactly the same size. Half of the Ten Commandments were engraved on each one.

These are the Ten Commandments:

1. I am *Hashem* your G-d, who took you out of Egypt.

2. Do not serve idols.

3. Do not swear falsely (in Hashem's name).

4. Keep the *Shabbat* day holy.

5. Honor your father and mother.

6. Do not murder.

7. Do not commit adultery.

8. Do not kidnap.

9. Do not be a false witness.

10. Do not be jealous of what other people have.

The last five commandments relate to the way we interact with others. How would you describe the first five?

613 Mitzvot
Rules to Live by

In the *Torah*, *Hashem* gives us 613 *mitzvot*. *Mitzvot* are commandments that relate to every part of our lives. Doing *mitzvot* helps us become better people. They show us how to serve *Hashem* and how to behave towards others. *Hashem* promises a reward for each *mitzvah* that we do, but the true reason we do *mitzvot* is simply because *Hashem* told us to. Doing what *Hashem* wants helps us connect to Him!

There are 248 positive *mitzvot* (things that we should do, like honor our parents) and 365 negative *mitzvot* (things that we must not do, like steal). Together, that adds up to 613 *mitzvot*.

Types of Mitzvot
Three Categories

There are three categories of *mitzvot*:

- **Eidot**: *Mitzvot* that commemorate miraculous events
  Example: Keeping *Pesach* (Passover), which reminds us of the exodus from Egypt

- **Mishpatim**: *Mitzvot* that make sense to us
  Example: The prohibition of murder

- **Chukim**: *Mitzvot* that we keep even though we don't understand the reasons behind them
  Example: Keeping milk and meat separate

Sheva Mitzvot
Commandments for Non-Jews

When *Hashem* created Adam, the first man, He gave him and his descendants six commandments to live by. If the people of the generations would have kept these laws, the world would have been filled with justice and peace.

Unfortunately, most people did not follow the path of truth. They became so wicked that *Hashem* destroyed them all in a great flood. Only Noach (Noah), the righteous man of those times, was chosen by *Hashem* to survive. Noach and his family took pairs from each type of creature in the world and loaded them into the gigantic wooden ship he built, called the *teivah*, or ark.

Seven for all mankind

After the flood, *Hashem* commanded Noach (Noah) to obey the six commandments that had been given to Adam, as well a seventh command. Noach and his family slowly reestablished the human race. Later, when *Hashem* gave the Jewish people the *Torah* at Mount Sinai, He also commanded the Jews to ensure that the non-Jewish nations of the world keep these seven laws.

The Noahide laws

1. Do not believe in or worship idols

2. Do not curse *Hashem*

3. Do not murder

4. Lead a moral family life

5. Do not steal

6. Establish courts of justice (to enforce these seven laws)

7. Do not eat meat taken from an animal while it was alive

Non-Jews who keep these seven laws because *Hashem* commanded them to are called the "Righteous Among the Nations of the World." They will be rewarded by *Hashem* and receive a portion in the World to Come.

TRY IT!

Do you have non-Jewish friends who might be interested in hearing about these seven laws? You can teach them!

Tanach
24 Books of the Torah

The *Torah* is a gift that *Hashem* gave us through Moshe on Mount Sinai. The *Torah* has two parts: the written *Torah* and the oral *Torah*.

The written Torah

Torah Shebichtav (the written part of the *Torah*) is made up of 24 books and is also called *Tanach*, a Hebrew acronym for its three sections: *Torah* (written by Moshe), *Nevi'im* (written by the prophets), and *Ketuvim* (written by various sages).

The oral Torah

The oral *Torah* is made up of explanations, teachings, and stories that were passed down verbally from Moshe and elaborated upon by our sages. These were later recorded in the *Mishnah* and the *Gemarah*.

There are many more holy books, written by very great rabbis, that are considered additional explanations on the *Torah*.

The following sections will describe the three parts of the written *Torah* and the tradition of the oral *Torah* in more detail.

Torah Shebichtav
The Written Torah

Who wrote it?

Moshe wrote the very first *Torah* scroll, recording *Hashem*'s exact words. Even the passages that refer to Moshe are written in the third person, because every word of it was dictated to him. Since then, every generation has trained scribes who write *Torah* scrolls by hand, with a quill and ink on parchment.

The Chumash

Today, we also have a printed copy of the first five books of the written *Torah*, called a *Chumash*. Because Moshe wrote the *Torah*, a *Chumash* is also called "The Five Books of Moses." The *Torah* scroll that the rabbi reads in synagogue and the printed *Chumash* that we learn from contain exactly the same words—and both were originally written by Moshe!

DID YOU KNOW?
The word *Chumash* literally means "five," for the number of books it contains.

What's inside?

The 613 *mitzvot* are written in the *Torah*, along with records of events occurring from the time of creation until just before the Jewish people entered the Land of Israel.

The five books of the Chumash

1. **Bereishit** (Genesis)
2. **Shemot** (Exodus)
3. **Vayikra** (Leviticus)
4. **Bamidbar** (Numbers)
5. **Devarim** (Deuteronomy)

The 54 parshiot

The *Chumash* is divided into 54 *Torah* portions, called *parshiot*. The weekly *parshah* is read aloud from a *Torah* scroll in *shul* (synagogue) on *Shabbat*. By the end of the year we will have finished reading the whole *Torah*—and then we start all over again!

DID YOU KNOW? Parts of the weekly *parsha* are also read on Monday, Thursday, and during the *Minchah* prayer on *Shabbat* afternoon.

Nevi'im
Prophets

This section includes eight books of the Prophets. They cover the period of time from Moshe's passing until the rebuilding of the second *Beit Hamikdash* (Holy Temple). The *Haftarah*, the *Torah* portion that is read in *shul* each week is taken from this section.

The prophets

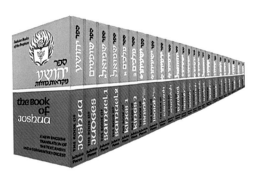

1. *Yehoshua* (Joshua)

2. *Shoftim* (Judges)

3. *Shmuel* (Samuel) *I & II*

4. *Melachim* (Kings) *I & II*

5. *Yirmiyahu* (Jeremiah)

6. *Yechezkel* (Ezekiel)

7. *Yeshayahu* (Isaiah)

8. *Trei Asar* (The Book of Twelve)
   This final book contains the prophecies of 12 prophets:

   - Hoshea
   - Yoel
   - Amos
   - Ovadiah
   - Yonah
   - Michah

   - Nachum
   - Chavakuk
   - Tzefaniah
   - Chaggai
   - Zechariah
   - Malachi

Ketuvim
Holy Writings

These "Holy Writings" are made up of 11 books. They are the last part of the written *Torah*. No further books can ever be added.

- *Rut* (Ruth)
- *Kohelet* (Ecclesiastes)
- *Tehillim* (Psalms)
- *Iyov* (Job)
- *Shir Hashirim* (Song of Songs)
- *Mishlei* (Proverbs)
- *Eichah* (Lamentations)
- *Ezra*
- *Nechemiah*
- *Daniel*
- *Esther*
- *Divrei Hayamim* (Chronicles) *I & II*

Torah Shebaal Peh
The Oral Torah

The oral *Torah* includes all the laws that Moshe learned from *Hashem* and transmitted verbally to his successors. The oral *Torah* includes the special traditions and rules for interpreting the written *Torah*. Without it, knowing how to do *mitzvot* would be impossible.

For example, we only know how *tefillin* should be made and worn because of the explanations given in the oral *Torah*.

The Mishnah

Many generations after Moshe, there was a great sage named Rabbi Yehudah Hanasi (Judah the Prince). He realized that due to growing hardships and persecutions, the Jews might not be able to remember all the laws and explanations of the oral *Torah* that had been passed down from generation to generation. He gathered the greatest scholars to organize and record every detail they had learned from their teachers. These writings were compiled into a set of books called the *Mishnah*.

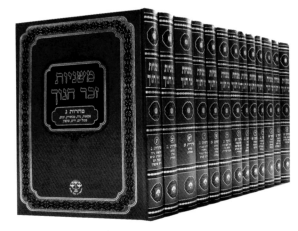

The sections

Rabbi *Yehudah Hanasi* divided the *Mishnah* into six general categories:

1. **Zera'im**: Laws of Agriculture and *Brachot* (Blessings)

---

2. **Mo'ed**: Laws of *Shabbat* and *Yom Tov (Holidays)*

---

3. **Noshim**: Laws of Marriage and Divorce

---

4. **Nezikin**: Laws of Damages, Property, and Justice

---

5. **Kodshim**: Laws of the *Beit Hamikdash* and *Kashrut*

---

6. **Taharot**: Laws of Purity and *Mikvah* (Ritual Bathing)

The *Mishnah* is the foundation of Jewish Law, preserving the *Torah* throughout history. Anything written about Jewish law after the *Mishnah* was completed is only a further explanation of its contents.

Gemarah

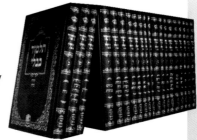

In later years, there were fewer rabbis who could understand the laws originally written in the *Mishnah* and teach them to the Jewish people. Even more explanations were needed to understand how to keep *mitzvot*. A body of discussion on the *Mishnah* was recorded, called the *Gemarah*, or *"Talmud."* In later generations, even the *Gemarah* became too difficult to understand, and the sages wrote additional commentaries to make it more accessible.

Shulchan Aruch

The *Gemarah* is full of back-and-forth discussions between rabbis. It soon became too difficult for less scholarly Jews to read through an entire argument before finally getting to the bottom line: how to keep *mitzvot*. To make this easier, Rabbi Yosef Cairo organized the final decisions into one set of books. He called his code of Jewish law the *Shulchan Aruch*, which literally means "set table," because the information of the *Gemarah* became as accessible as a prepared table of food.

The four sections:

1. *Orech Chaim:*
   Laws of Daily Life

2. *Yoreh De'ah:*
   Laws of Kosher Food
   and Purity

3. *Even Ha'ezer:*
   Laws of Marriage
   and Divorce

4. *Choshen Mishpat:*
   Laws of Business

Kabbalah

Since the beginning of creation, the Jewish people were blessed with great leaders, prophets, and sages who knew the *Torah's* deepest secrets. However, after the destruction of the *Beit Hamikdash* and the subsequent exile, such knowledge became increasingly rare. The Jews didn't have the peace of mind needed to delve into such deep concepts. Instead, they focused on learning Jewish law so that they would know how to serve *Hashem*. Only the most experienced scholars were able to comprehend the *Torah's* mystical secrets.

Still, even the simplest Jews retained their strong and pure belief in *Hashem*, and understood that He wanted them to learn *Torah* and do *mitzvot*.

Restoring the faith

As time went on and the exile became even more difficult, people's faith weakened. It was as if the Jewish people had fallen into a spiritual faint. However, in the 1500s, the sage Arizal said that the time had come to reveal the hidden wisdom of *Torah* and revitalize the Jews. He began teaching select students the mystical teachings of *Kabbalah*.

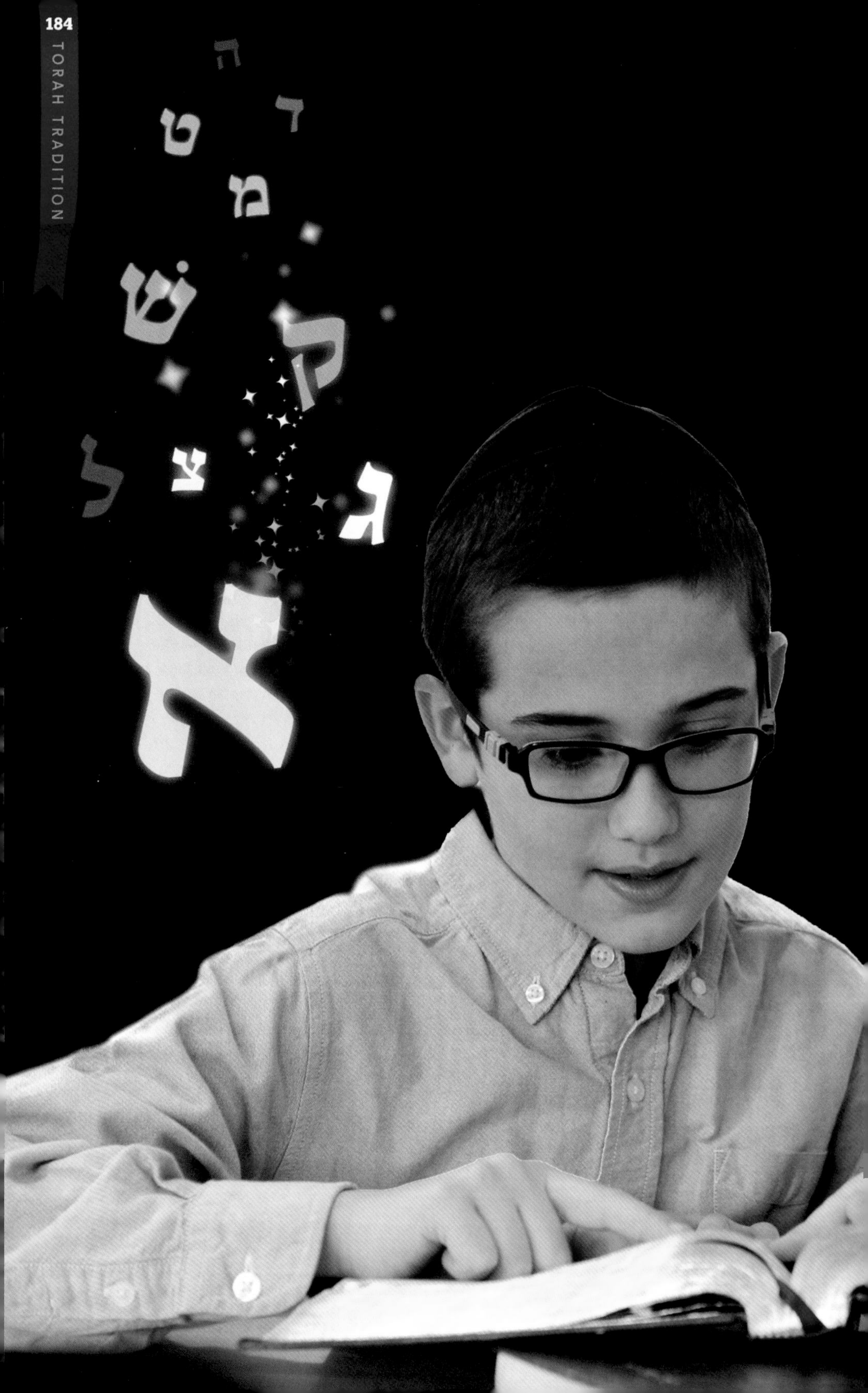
ה
ד
ט
מ
ש
ק
צ
ל
ג
א

Chassidut

The average person was still unable to study *Kabbalah*, since many of its ideas are very difficult to understand. The Baal Shem Tov changed all of this with the revelation of *Chassidut*, which explains the deepest ideas of *Kabbalah* in a manner that everyone can grasp. His student, the Magid of Mezritch, followed by the seven Chabad leaders, further developed these teachings.

Chassidut has been especially helpful in our generation, when many people question *Hashem's* existence. It has become necessary to reveal and spread these deep secrets of *Torah* in order to inspire Jews to keep their faith, prevent assimilation, and give us the strength to complete our service of *Hashem* in exile and bring *Mashiach*. Even children can learn *Chassidut* now, in the times before *Mashiach*.

SECTION 9

Jewish Heroes

Throughout our history, individuals have stood out as leaders, showing us how to conquer the world for *Hashem* (G-d). They are our role models—and you can be a Jewish hero too!

Note: The images used in this section are for illustrative purposes only, and they are not intended to accurately depict the holy faces of our ancestors.

Jewish Leaders
What it Takes

In every generation *Hashem* (G-d) blesses us with *tzadikim*—righteous, caring, and wise individuals who guide and uplift us. *Hashem*'s presence rests on these holy leaders.

Whether rich or poor, famous or humble, they are always selflessly committed to providing for the spiritual and material needs of the Jewish people. They are true examples of how to serve *Hashem* through learning *Torah* and following in its ways.

The greatest Jewish leader of all, whom we are all still waiting for, is *Mashiach* (the Messiah)!

Am Yisrael
A Nation is Born

The Jewish people have honorable ancestors: the *Avot*, or fathers, of the Jewish people are Avraham (Abraham), Yitzchak (Isaac), and Yaakov (Jacob). The *Imahot*, or mothers, are Sarah, Rivkah (Rebecca), Rachel, and Leah.

When we talk about any of these ancestors, we refer to them as *Avinu*, our father, or *Imeinu*, our mother. Our ancestors did everything they could to ensure that their children would continue in a good path. And just like physical children possess the genetic makeup of their parents, we are lucky to have inherited traits from our illustrious ancestors.

Avot and Imahot
The First Parents

Avraham, Yitzchak, and Yaakov merited to become the *Avot* of the Jewish people because they believed in *Hashem*, followed in His ways, and taught all the people around them to do so as well. *Hashem* appeared to each of our *Avot* because they were very righteous. Similarly, the *Imahot* of the Jewish people, Sarah, Rivkah, Rachel, and Leah, were extraordinary women who served *Hashem* with all of their hearts. *Hashem* trusted these great people to raise generations who would follow their examples and serve Him.

DID YOU KNOW?

All the Avot and Imahot of the Jewish nation, except for Rachel, are buried in *Ma'arat Hamachpelah* (the Cave of Machpelah) in Israel.

Avraham Avinu
Our Father Abraham

1813 BCE—1638 BCE

Avraham was the first Jew. At the young age of three, he recognized *Hashem* as the Creator of the entire universe.

Until Avraham's time, people served all different kinds of idols, believing that these statues had godly powers. People would bring offerings and pray to idols for rain, children, and other needs. In fact, Avraham's very father owned an idol store!

Avraham was the first to realize that these statues could not grant health or wealth. He tried convincing everyone else to serve *Hashem*. He even destroyed all the idols in his father's shop. King Nimrod was very upset at Avraham for believing in *Hashem* and for destroying idols, so he threw him into a fiery furnace. *Hashem* performed a miracle, and Avraham was able to walk through the flames unharmed. When people heard about this, they quickly realized that *Hashem* was the true Master of the universe. For the rest of his life, Avraham continued teaching others about *Hashem's* existence.

Avraham passed many tests, which showed his true belief in *Hashem*. *Hashem* promised that he would become the father of a great nation. After Avraham married Sarah, he and his wife followed *Hashem's* command and left their home to live in what would become the Land of Israel.

At the age of 99, Avraham circumcised himself as *Hashem* commanded. Even while in great pain afterward, he was still eager to welcome guests to his tent. When he was 100 years old, his son Yitzchak was born, who would continue his legacy.

Avraham passed away at the age of 175. He was buried next to his wife Sarah in *Ma'arat Hamachpelah,* in the city of Chevron (Hebron). This is where Adam and Chava (Eve) are also buried.

Claim to fame: true kindness

Avraham and Sarah were known for their generous hospitality. Their tent had entrances on all four sides so that travelers could easily enter from all directions. Avraham's kindness was so great that the Angel of Kindness complained to *Hashem* that since Avraham was born, he had no work to do in the world—Avraham did it all!

Sarah Imeinu
Our Mother Sarah

1803 BCE—1677 BCE

While Avraham taught the male visitors about *Hashem,* Sarah taught the females. *Hashem* told Avraham to listen to Sarah's advice, because she was a great prophetess—even greater than Avraham was! She did not have children for many years, then finally gave birth to Yitzchak at 90 years old. Sarah lived for 127 years. When she passed away, Avraham purchased *Ma'arat Hamachpelah* in Chevron. Sarah was the first of the *Avot* and *Imahot* to be buried there.

Claim to fame: miracles

Three notable events took place in Sarah's tent:

The *challah* she baked stayed fresh from week to week.	Her *Shabbat* candles remained lit from Friday to Friday.	A beautiful cloud of *Hashem's* Glory always hovered above her tent.

Yitzchak Avinu
Our Father Isaac

1713 BCE—1533 BCE

Yitzchak was born to his parents when they were 100 and 90 years old. Yitzchak was a great scholar and prophet. He married Rivkah, the second mother of the Jewish people. He lived until the age of 180.

Claim to fame: self-sacrifice

Yitzchak was famous for his courage; he was willing to give up his life for *Hashem*. When he was 37 years old, *Hashem* tested Avraham's faith by ordering him to bring his cherished son, Yitzchak, as an offering on Mount Moriah. Avraham did as he was commanded, and Yitzchak bravely offered himself to be bound for the sacrifice. At the last second, *Hashem* told Avraham not to kill his son—He had merely been testing his faith. Yet since Avraham was eager to carry out *Hashem's* instructions, *Hashem* considered it as though Avraham had actually fulfilled the command.

DID YOU KNOW?
Yitzchak became so holy through being offered as a sacrifice that he was never allowed to leave the Holy Land.

Rivkah Imeinu
Our Mother Rebecca

1677 BCE—1544 BCE

Rivkah's kind nature was evident from as early as three years old. When she met Avraham's servant, Eliezer, who had been sent to find a wife for Yitzchak, she offered to bring water for him and his ten camels. That's when Eliezer knew that Rivkah was the one for Yitzchak. Rivkah passed away at the age of 133.

Claim to fame: dealing with twins

When Rivkah was expecting, the prophets Shem and Ever told her that she would be the mother of two great nations, and that the older child would serve the younger one. Indeed, she gave birth to twin boys: Yaakov and Eisav. As her children grew older, Rivkah saw that Yaakov spent his time learning *Torah* and acted considerately toward others, while Eisav hunted all day long and was known for his wickedness. Rivkah made sure that Yaakov would inherit the spiritual legacy of his father instead of Eisav.

Yaakov Avinu
Our Father Jacob

1653 BCE—1506 BCE

Yaakov was the third of our *Avot*. He studied *Torah* diligently for many years in the Holy Land, and eventually left to dwell with his uncle Lavan (Laban). He married Lavan's daughters Rachel and Leah, as well as their two maidservants, Bilhah and Zilpah. Even while Yaakov lived with his wicked father-in-law, he kept all the laws of the *Torah*. Yaakov's 12 sons, all of whom were righteous, later became the 12 tribes of Israel. Yaakov lived for 147 years.

Claim to fame: Yisrael

On Yaakov's journey back to the Holy Land, the guardian angel of his wicked brother, Eisav, tried to strike him. The struggle lasted throughout the night, representing the essential battle of good against evil. When morning dawned, and the angel saw that he could not defeat Yaakov, he was forced to bless him. He also gave Yaakov the added name "Yisrael" (Israel). The Jews are called *"Bnei Yisrael,"* the Children of Israel, after this victory.

Leah Imeinu
Our Mother Leah

1591 BCE—1546 BCE

Leah is the third of the four *Imahot*. Leah was
Lavan's oldest daughter. When Yaakov wanted
to marry Leah's younger sister, Rachel, Lavan
tricked him into marrying Leah instead.

Claim to fame: her children

Leah is the mother of six of the 12 tribes and a daughter,
Dina. Leah's sons were Reuven (Ruben), Shimon (Simon),
Levi, Yehudah (Judah), Yissachar, and Zevulun (Zebulun). The
tribes of *Levi*, including the *Kohanim*, and of *Yehudah*—the
tribe of David Hamelech (King David) and *Mashiach*—both
descend from Leah.

Leah's maidservant, Zilpah, was also married to Yaakov.
She had two sons, Gad and Asher.

DID YOU KNOW?
In Biblical
times, it was
common for
a man to have
more than
one wife.

Rachel Imeinu
Our Mother Rachel

1591 BCE—1553 BCE

Rachel was the younger daughter of Yaakov's wicked uncle Lavan. She was also Yaakov's favorite wife. When Yaakov saw Rachel for the first time, he knew he was going to marry her. But Lavan tricked Yaakov: before the wedding, he switched Rachel with Leah. After first marrying Leah, Yaakov married Rachel seven days later.

Rachel was the mother of Yosef (Joseph) and Binyamin (Benjamin).Her maidservant, Bilhah, also married Yaakov and she had two sons, Dan and Naftali.

Claim to fame: gravesite power

Once 11 of his 12 children were born, Yaakov decided it was time to depart from Lavan's house and return to his homeland. On the journey to the Land of Israel, Rachel passed away while giving birth to Binyamin, the youngest of the 12 tribes. Yaakov buried Rachel on the roadside, just outside the city of Beit Lechem (Bethlehem). Her burial site is called *Kever Rachel.*

Years later, when Yosef was taken as a slave to Egypt, he prayed and wept at his mother's tomb. Centuries later, as thousands of Jews were led into Babylonian exile, they passed Rachel's gravesite and prayed there as well. Rachel's soul begged for mercy on behalf of her children, the nation of Israel. Her voice rose to *Hashem*'s throne, and *Hashem* listened to her prayers, promising that her children would eventually return to their land. Today, we still pray at *Kever Rachel*, asking *Hashem* to bless us in her merit.

The Twelve Tribes:
The Children of Israel

1. *Reuven*

2. *Shimon*

3. *Levi*

4. *Yehudah*

5. *Yissachar*

6. *Zevulun*

7. *Dan*

8. *Naftali*

9. *Gad*

10. *Asher*

11. *Yosef*

12. *Binyamin*

Yosef Hatzadik
Joseph the Righteous

1562 BCE—1452 BCE

Yosef was one of the 12 sons of Yaakov. His father loved him very much. As a young boy he had two symbolic dreams, each signifying that he would eventually become a ruler, the greatest among his brothers. In one dream, he saw the sun, moon, and 11 stars (symbolizing Yaakov, Leah, and his 11 brothers) bowing before him. When he shared his visions, his brothers became very jealous. Out of envy they sold him into slavery, and Yosef was taken down to Egypt. Over 20 years after having his dreams, Yosef became Pharaoh's second-in-command and indeed ruled over his brothers.

Claim to fame: standing strong

In Pharaoh's palace, Yosef was confronted with many sinful temptations. Despite this, he always overcame his *Yetzer Hara* (evil inclination) and remained righteous. Even within the corrupt and impure environment of Egypt, Yosef never forgot that he was a Jew. His two children, Menashe and Efraim, were born in Egypt and showed similar strength. They grew up to be faithful servants of *Hashem*.

Claim to fame: no grudge

When Yaakov's 11 sons came to Egypt to buy food during a famine, they didn't recognize their little brother, who had become a great and mighty ruler. Once Yosef revealed his identity, they were afraid that he would take revenge on them for having sold him, but Yosef forgave his brothers wholeheartedly. He brought the entire family to Egypt, where he took care of all of their needs.

Moshe Rabbeinu
Moses Our Teacher

1393 BCE—1273 BCE

Moshe was the greatest of all prophets. He was born in Egypt at a time when Pharaoh had decreed that all Jewish boys must be killed. Moshe's mother, Yocheved, hid him from the Egyptians and placed him in a basket on the Nile River. Pharaoh's daughter, Batya, discovered him there and decided to raise him in the palace as her own son. Despite his unusual upbringing, Moshe never forgot that he was a Jew. As an adult, he saw an Egyptian taskmaster beating a Jewish slave. He killed the Egyptian to save the Jew and escaped to Midyan, where *Hashem* spoke to him from a burning bush.

Claim to fame: Egyptian Exodus

Hashem told Moshe to go to Egypt and order Pharaoh to free the Jewish people. Moshe followed *Hashem*'s instructions, bringing ten plagues upon Egypt until the Jewish people were finally allowed to leave. He led the Jews out of Egypt and through the *Yam Suf* (Sea of Reeds), which miraculously split, allowing the Jews to walk through dry land. Moshe received the

Luchot (Tablets) with the Ten Commandments at Mount Sinai and taught *Torah* to the Jewish people. That's why we call him "*Rabbeinu*," our teacher.

Claim to fame: leadership

Moshe led the Jews through 40 years of wandering in the desert. At last our nation stood at the borders of the Promised Land. Moshe's deepest desire was to enter, but *Hashem* had decreed that it was not to be. Instead, Moshe's student Yehoshua (Joshua) would lead the way. Before Moshe passed on, at 120 years of age, *Hashem* showed him what would happen to the Jewish people in the years to come.

"I know that I cannot enter the land," Moshe told *Hashem*. "Therefore, I beg of You to bless the Jewish people with wise and patient leaders."

"Moshe," *Hashem* replied, "My nation will have many great rabbis, judges, and prophets. But only one will be as righteous as you ask: he will be the last redeemer, *Mashiach*."

Aharon Hakohen
Faithful Servant

1396 BCE—1274 BCE

Aharon was Moshe's older brother. He was a prophet and the first *kohen gadol*, given the honor of serving in the Holy Temple. Every *Kohen* descends from Aharon.

Aharon was also the one who helped Moshe communicate with Pharaoh when the Jews were slaves in Egypt.

Claim to fame: peacemaker

Aharon was known for his pursuit of harmony and his efforts to resolve quarrels and spread brotherly love.

Miriam Haneviah
Miriam the Prophetess

1399 BCE—1274 BCE

Miriam, the sister of Moshe and Aharon, was a great prophetess.

Claim to fame: prophecy

As a little girl, when Egyptian slavery was at its worst, Miriam predicted that her parents would give birth to a baby who would redeem the Jewish people. Soon after, her brother Moshe was born. Miriam watched over him when he was placed in a basket on the Nile River. Soon after, once he was discovered and adopted by Pharaoh's daughter, Miriam made sure that baby Moshe would only nurse from a Jewish woman.

Claim to fame: song and dance

At the crossing of the *Yam Suf* as the Jews left Egypt, Miriam led the women in a song of praise for *Hashem*'s miracles.

Claim to fame: the well

During the 40 years that they wandered through the desert, the Jewish people drew water from a miraculous well that followed them wherever they went. When Miriam died, the well disappeared. Everyone then realized that the water had only flowed in her merit.

Yehoshua ben Nun
Joshua

1355 BCE—1245 BCE

Yehoshua was Moshe's special student and a prophet, who became the leader of the Jewish people after Moshe's passing. He led the Jewish people into the Promised Land and divided territories among the tribes of Israel according to a lottery decided by *Hashem*. He was a leader and judge of Israel until his death at the age of 110.

Claim to fame: miracle victory

With *Hashem*'s help, Yehoshua led the nation to conquer the city of Yericho, the first battle fought to settle the land of Israel. After seven days of circling the city, seven *kohanim* blew seven trumpets and the walls of the city miraculously fell.

Devorah Haneviah
Deborah the Prophetess

Devorah was a judge of the Jewish people. She would sit outdoors so that both women and men would feel comfortable approaching her. Although she was a public figure, she always conducted herself in a modest way.

Claim to fame: a song

When the Jewish general Barak waged war against the Jews' enemies, he asked Devorah to accompany the army. He was sure that having a righteous prophetess with them would help assure their triumph. The Jewish army was victorious, and Devorah composed a celebratory song, recorded in the Book of Judges. After the victory, the Jewish people lived in peace for the next 40 years.

Rut
Ruth

Rut was a righteous convert to Judaism. When her husband died she returned to the Holy Land with her mother-in-law, Naomi, and swore allegiance to *Hashem* and to the Jewish people. She married Boaz, who was the judge of Israel at the time.

Claim to fame: a great-grandson

Rut met her husband Boaz while gathering fallen grain from his field. She gave birth to David Hamelech's (King David's) grandfather. All Jewish kings, including *Mashiach*, descend from her.

Chana Haneviah
Hannah the Prophetess

For many years Chana did not have any children. She constantly prayed to *Hashem* to grant her a son, whose life she promised to dedicate to holy service. Eli, the *kohen gadol*, once saw her praying quietly, whispering the words with great feeling. Because people in those days usually prayed aloud, he scolded her, assuming she was drunk. Chana explained that she was praying for a child from the depth of her heart. Once Eli understood, he gave her a blessing that *Hashem* would answer her prayers.

Our Sages say that we learn from Chana to pray with feeling. We also learn to bless someone if we accuse them wrongly, and to explain the truth if someone misjudges us.

Claim to fame: sacrifice

Chana was the mother of one of our greatest prophets, Shmuel. When he was two years old, she brought him to the *kohen gadol* so that he could serve *Hashem* in the *Mishkan* (Tabernacle). Shmuel grew up working there, and eventually he became a leader of the Jewish people.

Shmuel Hanavi
Samuel the Prophet

929 BCE—877 BCE

Shmuel was a great prophet and the last of the biblical judges. He was the son of Elkanah and Chana, who brought him to Eli, the *kohen gadol*, to be raised in the *Mishkan*. After Eli died, Shmuel was appointed as a prophet of *Hashem*. Shmuel lived for 52 years and is buried just northwest of Jerusalem.

Claim to fame: crowning kings

After Shmuel was appointed prophet, the Jews protested that they wanted a king like other nations had. Following *Hashem*'s command, Shmuel anointed Shaul (Saul), who was from the tribe of *Binyamin*, as the first king of Israel. But King Shaul did not follow *Hashem*'s commandment: he allowed the king of Amalek, a sworn enemy of the Jewish people, to remain alive. Shmuel then slew the enemy king himself and informed King Shaul that the kingship would be given to someone more worthy. *Hashem* told Shmuel to go to the city of Beit Lechem (Bethlehem) and anoint a new king: David.

David Hamelech
King David

907 BCE—837 BCE

David was a shepherd who later became king of Israel. The care and concern that he showed for every individual sheep convinced *Hashem* that David would take similar care of His People. David was the youngest of his father's seven sons. While he was still very young, *Hashem* commanded the Prophet Shmuel to anoint David as king. Later, David served as King Shaul's armor-bearer and played harp for him.

Claim to fame: defeated Goliath

The Philistines wanted to wage war with the Jews. They challenged them to a duel with Goliath, their greatest warrior. Only David bravely accepted—no one else dared face the mighty giant, who stood over 12 feet tall and was clad in heavy copper armor. Though everyone ridiculed him, David assured them that just like *Hashem* had helped him fight off the wild animals that attacked his sheep, Hashem would now help the young shepherd vanquish the Philistine. David took his shepherd's staff, a sling, and five smooth stones and descended to the valley between the Philistine and

Jewish camps. When Goliath saw a young boy representing the Jewish people, he threatened to swallow David alive. But *Hashem* helped David, and the young shepherd struck down the giant with a well-aimed stone. With their leader dead, the Philistines were completely powerless. This was the beginning of David's legacy as a great hero, conqueror, and king of Israel.

Claim to fame: Tehillim

To David, *Hashem* was not only great and mighty, but also dear and beloved. David spoke to Him as one would speak to a close friend, sharing all of his deepest thoughts and feelings. David composed many beautiful songs for *Hashem*. These praises are written in the book of *Tehillim* (Psalms), which is one of the most important sources of prayer for all Jews.

Claim to fame: ancestor of Mashiach

You might know the song, "*David, melech Yisrael, chai chai v'kayom*," which means, "David, King of Israel, is alive and lives on." *Hashem* promised David that royalty will forever belong to him and his descendants. His dynasty will culminate with *Mashiach*, who is called "son of David."

Eliyahu Hanavi
Elijah the Prophet

Eliyahu was a prophet who lived in Israel during the reign of the evil King Achav (Ahab), when idol worship had spread among the Jews. Despite King Achav's attempts to stop him, Eliyahu fought to strengthen the nation's belief in *Hashem*. When Eliyahu spoke out against Achav's right to be king, he was exiled. In the course of his journeys, he performed many miracles.

Claim to fame: battling the Ba'al

The most famous idol of those times was called the "*Ba'al.*" Eliyahu fought very hard against this form of idol worship, which many Jews had unfortunately begun to serve. He offered to hold a public competition to prove that there is only one *Hashem*: he and the priests of *Ba'al* would each offer a sacrifice and the animal consumed by heavenly fire would prove the true G-d.

Eliyahu gathered all the Jews on Mount Carmel and demanded: "How long will you waver between two sides? If *Hashem* is G-d, follow Him; and if *Ba'al* is the truth, follow him!" The prophets of *Ba'al* placed their sacrifice on an altar, but could not cause a fire to descend from heaven. After Eliyahu's prayer, however, a miraculous fire came down from heaven and consumed his offering. All who were watching cried out, "*Hashem* is G-d!"

Claim to fame: eternal life

Hashem commanded Eliyahu to anoint Elisha as the next prophet. When the time came for Eliyahu to depart from this world, Elisha begged him to stay. They walked to the city of Yericho (Jericho), where Elisha requested that Eliyahu's power of prophecy be transferred to him. Eliyahu replied, "Only if you can see me as I am taken upward."

Suddenly, a fiery chariot appeared, and Eliyahu went up to heaven alive.

Claim to fame: mysterious sightings

Since Eliyahu never died, many stories have been told of his reappearance. It is said that he often appears in times of need or danger to help Jews. During the Talmudic Age, he taught secrets of *Torah* to some of the sages, who went on to write important books. Eliyahu has also appeared to great sages and *tzadikim* (righteous people) in more recent generations. According to tradition, Eliyahu is also present at every *brit milah* (circumcision) and *Pesach* (Passover) *Seder*.

Claim to fame: Passover cup

In the future, Eliyahu will give definitive rulings on questions in Jewish law that have remained undecided. The *Torah* tells us that Eliyahu will appear to herald the true and complete redemption when *Mashiach* comes. We demonstrate how much we long for this era by placing a fifth cup of wine on the Passover *Seder* table, which we call "Eliyahu's cup."

Mordechai and Esther Heroes of Purim

Under the rule of King Achashverosh in the Persian empire, the wicked minister Haman plotted to kill all the Jews on the 13th day of the Jewish month of *Adar*. At the last moment, *Hashem* sent salvation to His nation through Queen Esther and her cousin Mordechai, who were the leaders of the Jewish people at the time. That's why we celebrate the holiday of *Purim*.

Claim to fame: Jewish pride

Mordechai was always faithful to his people and to the *Torah*. When King Achashverosh's soldiers searched all over the country for a suitable new queen, Mordechai tried to hide Esther so she wouldn't have to go to the palace and marry a non-Jew.

Mordechai strengthened the Jewish people by teaching *Torah* to thousands of Jewish children. He also worked with Esther to make Haman's evil plot fail. After Haman was killed, Mordechai became the king's new advisor.

Esther was one of the seven prophetesses. She was
beautiful and modest at the same time. Even while living in
Achashverosh's palace, she observed *Shabbat* and ate only
kosher food. It was Esther who advised the Jews to find
favor in *Hashem's* eyes through fasting. She risked her life
by appearing before Achashverosh to try and save the Jews
from Haman's wicked plan. The scroll of the *Purim* story (from
which we read twice on the holiday) is called *Megillat Esther*
in her honor.

The Maccabees
Heroes of Chanukah

Mattisyahu (Mattathias), the son of Yochanan, the *kohen gadol*, lived in the village of Modi'in, not too far from Jerusalem. When Syrian–Greek rulers forbade the Jews from studying *Hashem*'s *Torah* or keeping His *mitzvot*, Mattisyahu and his five sons (the *Maccabees*) decided to fight against their powerful army. It is because of their bravery that we celebrate *Chanukah*.

Read more about the holidays of *Purim* and *Chanukah* in Section 5.

Claim to fame: victory

Yehudah (Judah), Mattisyahu's son, led all the Jews who were loyal to *Hashem's Torah*. On their shields they engraved the word "*Maccabees*," an acronym of their motto, "*Mi Kamocha Ba'eilim Hashem*—Who is like You amongst the mighty, *Hashem*?" With *Hashem*'s help, the handful of untrained *Maccabee* soldiers succeeded in defeating the mighty Syrian–Greek army.

Yehudit
Hero of Chanukah

Claim to fame: saving the day

A heroine of the *Chanukah* story, Yehudit helped the Jews defeat wicked tyrants during the fierce battles against the Syrian-Greeks. She allowed herself to be captured and taken to an enemy general's tent. The clever and beautiful Yehudit offered him an abundance of salty cheese and wine. The wicked man became drunk, promptly falling into a deep sleep. Yehudit courageously drew the sword hanging from his belt and cut off his head. She escaped and hung the head up on a high wall outside the camp. The next morning, when the Syrian–Greek soldiers saw that their general had been murdered, they were terrified. They fled from the front lines, and the Jews were victorious!

Rabbi Akiva
Scholarly Shepherd

Circa 16 CE—Circa 136 CE

Rabbi Akiva was one of the greatest Jewish sages. He lived during the era of the second *Beit Hamikdash*. The *Gemarah* often comments on his many good traits. Rabbi Akiva, who himself was poor, spent a great deal of time traveling with his colleagues to gather funds for other poor people. He even gave away many of his own possessions to needy students. A knowledgeable and dedicated scholar, he was a master of both Jewish law and the secrets of *Torah*.

Claim to fame: never too old

Until the age of 40, Akiva worked as a shepherd for Kalba Savua, one of the wealthiest Jews at the time. He was completely ignorant of *Torah*. One day, while Akiva was sitting by a stream, he saw drops of water dripping onto a stone, carving a hole through it. He realized that if soft water could make a hole in a hard rock, surely the strong words of *Torah* could penetrate his mind. He, too, would learn *Torah*!

Claim to fame: supportive wife

Kalba Savua wanted his daughter Rachel to marry someone of high social status. But a scholarly husband was more important to her, so when the poor shepherd Akiva promised to devote himself to *Torah*-learning, she married him. Kalba Savua did not approve of the marriage and denied customary financial support. Rachel endured great poverty to enable her husband to become a scholar. After 24 years of study, Rabbi Akiva returned home, accompanied by thousands of students. "We owe all of our learning to her," he told them.

Claim to fame: brilliant mind

Rabbi Akiva's great wisdom enabled him to interpret the meaning of every word in the *Torah*, even those which, at first glance, seem to have only a simple explanation. Both Jewish and non-Jewish scholars from all over the world consulted with him, always impressed by his great wisdom.

Claim to fame: valiant death

Rabbi Akiva was also a patriotic leader. He stood by Bar Kochba, who led a rebellion against the Roman leaders oppressing the Jewish people. When their uprising failed, the Romans tried to stamp out all *Torah* learning. Rabbi Akiva was thrown into prison and sentenced to death. Even from his prison cell, Rabbi Akiva continued to teach his students— some of whom would come to see him in disguise. While the Romans tortured him, he demonstrated great courage for *Torah*, using his last breath on this earth to proclaim "*Shema Yisrael*" with all of his heart. When his soul left his body, a voice from Heaven called out: "Fortunate are you, Akiva! You are destined to live forever in the World to Come."

Rabbi Shimon bar Yochai
Teacher of Kabbalah

Rabbi Shimon, also called the "Rashbi," was born in northern Israel. His father, Yochai, who was highly respected at the imperial court in Rome, sent his son to become a scholar at the school of Rabbi Gamliel and Rabbi Yehoshua. The most notable of Rabbi Shimon's teachers was Rabbi Akiva, under whom he studied for 13 years. He even stayed with his teacher in prison so that they could continue their study sessions.

Claim to fame: resisting oppression

Rabbi Shimon bar (son of) Yochai openly voiced his hatred for the Roman oppression. As a result, he was forced to hide in a cave for 13 years. There, while living on carob fruit from a tree that grew miraculously and water from a nearby stream, he studied with his son, Rabbi Elazar. As an old man, he traveled to government headquarters in Rome and successfully pleaded on behalf of the Jewish people.

Claim to fame: Lag B'omer

Rabbi Shimon *bar* Yochai passed away on the 18th of *Iyar* and was buried in the city of Meron, near Tzfat. He asked

that the day of his passing be observed forever as one of rejoicing. Thousands of Jews visit his gravesite every *Lag B'Omer* to celebrate.

Claim to fame: the Zohar

The Rashbi was one of the most eminent sages of *Kabbalah*, the inner secrets of the *Torah*. He wrote his teachings in the *Zohar*, a central work on the study of *Kabbalah*.

Rabbi Yehudah Hanasi
Our Holy Master

120—190 CE

The Jewish people called Rabbi Yehudah Hanasi (the Prince) simply by the title "Rebbi," our teacher, because he was more instrumental than any other sage in keeping the teachings of *Torah* alive. In addition to his constant study of Jewish subjects, Rabbi Yehudah Hanasi also became an expert in scientific fields, applying this knowledge to Jewish Law.

As Yehudah grew up, he studied under the guidance of the greatest sages of his time, including Rabbi Shimon bar Yochai. Both his family background and personal achievements prepared him to become one of the greatest Jewish leaders.

Claim to fame: sacrifice

When Rabbi Yehudah was born, his father risked his life to circumcise him, because the Romans had decreed that any Jews who circumcised their children would be put to death.

Claim to fame: government

Since Rabbi Yehudah spoke Latin and Greek fluently, he was able to take many trips to Rome, where he could plead Jewish causes before the Roman court without the help of an interpreter. The great esteem that the Romans had for Rabbi Yehudah brought many benefits to the Jewish people.

Claim to fame: leadership

Because of his great knowledge, noble descent, and considerable wealth, Rabbi Yehudah was unanimously elected president of the *Sanhedrin* (Jewish Supreme Court). However, his high position never lessened his great humility.

Claim to fame: the Mishnah

The most important accomplishment of this great sage was the compilation of the *Mishnah*, containing a wealth of information that, until then, had only been passed down orally from teacher to student. Rabbi Yehudah Hanasi collected, organized, and edited the entire oral *Torah*, writing it down in simple Hebrew, so that its contents would not be lost over time. These six volumes became the foundation of Jewish practice. Because of this accomplishment, as well as his other positive qualities, Rabbi Yehudah Hanasi is also called *Rabbeinu Hakadosh* or "Our Holy Master."

Rashi
Rabbi Shlomo Yitzchaki

1040—1105 CE

Rabbi Shlomo Yitzchaki, famously known as "Rashi," lived in France and earned his living as a winemaker. He was a descendant of David Hamelech (King David) and the greatest teacher of his time.

Claim to fame: illuminating Torah

Rashi put together a comprehensive commentary of the *Torah* that is studied by every student who learns *Chumash*, *Navi*, or *Gemarah*.

Even though his commentary is simple and concise, the deepest levels of meaning are contained in its words. Rashi's commentary on the *Torah* is often referred to as the "Wine of *Torah*," because it squeezes rich meaning out of even seemingly straightforward text, just like wine is squeezed from grapes.

Maimonides
Rabbi Moshe ben Maimon

1138—1204 CE

Rabbi Moshe ben Maimon, the "Rambam," or "Maimonides," as he is more commonly called, was a brilliant scholar, dedicated physician, prolific author, and respected *Torah* leader. He was born in Spain and later lived in North Africa during a period of Spanish religious persecution. He earned his living as a doctor and served as the personal physician to the sultan of Egypt.

From morning to night, the Rambam toiled on behalf of his suffering people. A descendent of David Hamelech, he was the greatest Jewish leader of his time. His gravestone in Tiveria (Tiberias), Israel, reads, "From Moshe [Rabbeinu (our teacher, Moses)] until Moshe [the Rambam], there never arose another like Moshe."

Claim to fame: influential author

The Rambam wrote many books, including medical and scientific journals. He detailed the Thirteen Principles of Faith, which are the foundations of Jewish belief. He also wrote an explanation of the *Mishnah* and composed *Sefer Hamitzvot* (Book of Commandments), giving a short overview of each of the 613 commandments. His greatest work is called *Yad Hachazaka* (The Mighty Arm), which is a series of 14 books explaining the Torah's laws. The Rambam's contribution to Jewish literature electrified the Jewish world during his lifetime and continues to influence world Jewry in modern times.

For the Thirteen Principles of Faith, see page 153.

Nachmanides
Rabbi Moshe ben Nachman

1194—1270 CE

Rabbi Moshe ben (son of) Nachman, known by his acronym "Ramban," *or* "Nachmanides," was an extraordinary Jewish leader who lived in Spain. At a very young age, he was already recognized for his vast knowledge and deep understanding of the *Torah*. A great master of

Kabbalah, the Ramban also wrote brilliant commentaries on the *Gemarah* and *Chumash*, which inspire *Torah* students to this very day. Later in life, he left Spain because of persecution and settled in the Land of Israel, where he opened a distinguished *yeshivah* (school of *Torah* study).

Claim to fame: gifted with logic

The Ramban loved his people and fought courageously for them. When the Jews were threatened with forced conversion, he came to their defense. In a public debate between representatives of Judaism and Christianity, presided over by the king of Spain, the Ramban's strong arguments proved the truth of Judaism.

Beit Yosef
Rabbi Yosef Cairo

1488—1575 CE

Rabbi Yosef Cairo, also known as the "Beit Yosef," grew up during the Spanish Inquisition, a time of harsh persecution for the Jews. He and his family suffered as they fled from country to country.

Claim to fame: the Shulchan Aruch

As Yosef grew older, he saw how Jews were losing touch with tradition and forgetting the precious teachings of the *Torah*. What could be done? The *Torah* was so vast, its laws numerous and detailed. How would the Jewish people ever be able to remember everything in the difficult conditions of their exile?

He knew that if he did not succeed in teaching the *Torah* to the Jewish people again, it might be forever forgotten. Rabbi Yosef set himself to the monumental task of writing a basic and straightforward text, a code of Jewish law. He hoped that this book would strengthen the Jewish people's observance of *mitzvot*.

For many years, Rabbi Yosef worked day and night, organizing all the laws of the *Torah* and writing them down in a clear and easy-to-understand manner. He called this work the *Shulchan Aruch* (the Set Table). The *Shulchan Aruch* is a central guidebook for Jews everywhere, teaching us how *Hashem* wants us to live our lives.

The Arizal
Rabbi Yitzchak Luria

1534—1572 CE

Rabbi Yitzchak Luria, known as the "Arizal," was a great *tzaddik* and master of *Kabbalah*. Very little is known about his early life, except that he was raised by his grandfather. When he arrived in Tzfat, Israel, in 1570, he was already recognized as a great sage.

Claim to fame: spiritual secrets

The Arizal taught *Kabbalah*, the deepest secrets of the *Torah*, to a small group of students. Until the times of the Arizal, these mystical secrets were studied only by experienced scholars.

The Baal Shem Tov
Rabbi Yisrael Baal Shem

1698—1760 CE

Rabbi Yisrael, later known as the "Baal Shem Tov," was the founder of the Chassidic movement. He was orphaned at a young age, and his father's parting words before passing away were, "Fear no one but *Hashem* and love every Jew with all of your heart." This was how the Baal Shem Tov lived his life, and how he taught others to live as well.

Claim to fame: thank G-d!

The Baal Shem Tov used to stop people and ask about the welfare of their families, businesses, and animals just to accustom them to praise *Hashem* constantly. He showed love to all Jews, regardless of background. He uplifted the many uneducated Jews of his time by explaining how precious they were to *Hashem*.

Claim to fame: meeting Mashiach

The Baal Shem Tov was a righteous and holy scholar who made the teachings of *Kabbalah* accessible to the simplest Jews. He was also known for his many miracle stories. Once, the Baal Shem Tov's soul went up to heaven, where he saw *Mashiach*. He asked him when he would come to redeem the Jewish people. *Mashiach* answered, "When your teachings of *Chassidut* are spread throughout the world."

The Alter Rebbe
Rabbi Shneur Zalman of Liadi

1745—1812 CE

Rabbi Shneur Zalman of Liadi, known as the "Alter Rebbe," was a direct descendant of David Hamelech (King David). The Alter Rebbe led his thousands of *Chassidim* (devoted followers) in the ways of the Baal Shem Tov. He was the founder of *Chabad Chassidut* and the first in the dynasty of the *Chabad leaders.*

Claim to fame: two lights

The Alter Rebbe was a master of both the revealed and inner teachings of the *Torah.* He compiled an updated version of the *Shulchan Aruch* (the code of Jewish law) to make it easier to use. His greatest work is called the "*Tanya.*" It explains how every Jew can serve *Hashem* wholeheartedly.

Claim to fame: imprisonment

At one point in his life, the Alter Rebbe was arrested by the Russian government on false charges and spent 53 days in prison. The 53 days are said to correspond to the 53 chapters of the *Tanya.*

Ben Ish Chai
Rabbi Yosef Chaim

1835—1909 CE

Rabbi Yosef Chaim, otherwise known as the "Ben Ish Chai," was a remarkably gifted child whose fame spread far and wide while he was still young. He was a genius in *Torah* and very careful in keeping *mitzvot*. When he grew up, he became the *Torah* leader of Baghdad's community. Scholars of all backgrounds turned to him with their questions. The Ben Ish Chai taught the *Sefardic* Jews of Iraq, Syria, North Africa, and Israel. He was not only a giant in the wisdom of the revealed *Torah*, but also a teacher of its inner meaning as well. He wrote at length about practical Jewish law. Today, most of the *Sefardic* Jews around the world follow his rulings on Jewish tradition.

Claim to fame: a good host

The Ben Ish Chai is known to have been a very modest person, loved by all who knew him. His home was open to all hungry people, and he would make sure to serve his visitors personally, even preparing comfortable beds for those in need of rest.

Claim to fame: bringing Jews closer

The Ben Ish Chai was a holy man who influenced countless Jews to come closer to *Hashem*. His lectures were attended by the entire community: rabbis and laymen, women and children. His sermons were always full of fascinating stories with lessons on how to serve *Hashem*. Great rabbis would rise at the mention of his name, and young and old, male and female, could quote his teachings by heart.

The Chofetz Chaim
Rabbi Yisrael Meir Hakohen

1839—1933 CE

Rabbi Yisrael Meir *Hakohen* Kagan, known as the "Chofetz Chaim," was a gentle and humble man. He wrote scholarly books on Jewish law, as well as volumes for women, young students, and uneducated Jewish soldiers serving in the Russian army. He taught about the importance of cleanliness and the giving of *tzedakah* (charity). He also established free loan funds for the poor.

Claim to fame: anti-gossip

He is called the "Chofetz Chaim" after his book he on the laws of speech. With it, he began a campaign against *lashon hara* (negative talk about other people), because he felt that the issue was a main source of strife for the Jewish nation.

Claim to fame: Mashiach clothes

Throughout his long life, the Chofetz Chaim worked to prepare himself and his generation for *Mashiach*. He wrote essays and books about the future redemption. He felt that the time for *Mashiach* was near. So whenever he traveled, he carried a special garment to wear in honor of *Mashiach*'s arrival. He founded a *yeshivah* in Jerusalem for *kohanim* to study the laws of the *Beit Hamikdash*, so that they would be ready to begin their duties as soon as *Mashiach* came.

The Frierdiker Rebbe
The Previous Rebbe

1880—1950 CE

The sixth *Chabad Rebbe*, Rabbi Yosef Yitzchak Schneerson, founded the *Chabad* movement in America. After he escaped Nazi-occupied Europe and arrived on the shores of United States, Rabbi Yosef Yitzchak was determined to create a new center of *Torah* in the United States. During a decade of dedicated work in the face of discouragement, he laid the foundation for the rich Jewish life that exists in America today. Rabbi Yosef Yitzchak Schneerson, who is also called the "Previous Rebbe," passed away in 1950 on the tenth day of *Shvat*. He was succeeded by his son-in-law, Rabbi Menachem Mendel Schneerson, our *Rebbe*.

Claim to fame: prison stay

An unrelenting champion of Jews and Judaism in Communist Russia, Rabbi Yosef Yitzchak Schneerson encouraged his *shluchim* (messengers) to keep Judaism alive in the Soviet Union despite all odds. His dedication in the face of oppression inspired many others to action. Because of his efforts to strengthen Judaism, he was imprisoned, tortured, and sentenced to death by the Communist government. His sentence was soon modified to exile and eventually dismissed completely. He was notified of his freedom on the 12th of *Tammuz*, his birthday, and was released the next day, on the 13th of *Tammuz*. He wrote that this freedom had brought redemption not only to himself, but to every Jew, and that these days were cause for celebration.

Rabbi Moshe Feinstein
A Torah Authority

1895—1986 CE

A renowned and important Jewish scholar of modern times, Rabbi Moshe Feinstein was a gentle and pious man. He was a master of the Jewish law and wrote many books explaining how to faithfully observe *mitzvot* in modern times. He was a great *Torah* authority and answered many of the most complicated questions of Jewish law in the modern era.

Claim to fame: playing "study"

When he was barely seven years old, young Moshe loved to learn more than anything else. "That is how I have fun," he explained. While other children played "house," he made up memory games with his brothers to see how well they had learned their lessons. By the age of eight, he had learned the entire written *Torah*. As he grew older, he learned the entire oral *Torah* as well.

Claim to fame: considering questions

All kinds of Jews would turn to Rabbi Moshe with questions. Even children used to come for advice. When someone would approach him with even the most simple question, he always took it seriously and gave the person time and respect, as if he had never heard the question before.

Baba Sali
Rabbeinu Yisrael Abuchatzeirah

1889—1984 CE

Rabbeinu Yisrael Abuchatzeirah, called the "Baba Sali," descended from a long line of famous *Torah* scholars. He took over his father's position as head of a *yeshivah* and rabbi of the Moroccan community before eventually moving to Israel. He became a master of *Kabbalah* and developed close relationships with many great rabbis.

Claim to fame: blessings

When the Baba Sali was young, his father told him, "I see that you have a special power to bless people. From now on, you must say good things." Young Yisrael promised that he would. Soon it became known that the blessings of this child brought miraculous results.

Thousands of Jews, and many non-Jews as well, came from all over the world to seek his advice and receive coins from him to give to *tzedakah* (charity).

Claim to fame: humility

Although he regularly gave many *Torah* lectures, the Baba Sali did not permit his students to write down his teachings. He was very humble and did not want to attract attention. Despite these efforts, his prophetic powers and miraculous prayers became world-renowned.

The Rebbe
Leader of Our Generation

The Lubavitcher Rebbe, world leader of the *Chabad-Lubavitch* movement, has been described as the most dynamic Jewish personality of our time. Famous for his tremendous knowledge of *Torah* and his love for all Jews, he breathed the spirit of Judaism back into the Jewish people. The *Rebbe* reached out to Jews everywhere with special *mivtzoim* (campaigns), founded numerous institutions to strengthen Jewish observance, and sent thousands of *shluchim* (emissaries) to establish Jewish centers around the world. The *Rebbe* is our generation's most influential Jewish leader.

Claim to fame: self-sacrifice

From a young age, the *Rebbe* displayed a selfless love for his people. As a child in Russia, he distributed candies to other terrified children while they hid together in a dark cellar to escape a pogrom (violent attack on Jews). Later, at age nine, he jumped into the Black Sea to save a boy from drowning. His self-sacrifice was matched by his scholarship, apparent from childhood, as he possessed a legendary memory and incredible intellect.

> **DID YOU KNOW?**
> Tzivos Hashem is one of the many *Torah* institutions that the *Rebbe* founded.
>
>

Claim to fame: the Rebbetzin

The *Rebbe's* wife, Rebbetzin Chaya Mushka, was the daughter of the sixth *Chabad Rebbe*. She was highly educated in *Torah*, and it is said that she anonymously authored several Jewish works. She was a very

modest woman and realized all of her great achievements in a quiet and discreet manner. Throughout the years, the *Rebbetzin* assisted the *Rebbe* in his tireless efforts on behalf of *Torah* and the Jewish people.

Claim to fame: Mashiach preparations

The *Rebbe* is recognized throughout the world as a *tzadik* who can foretell the future and whose blessings will come true. He proclaimed that ours is the last generation of exile, and that we are living in the first generation of *geulah* (redemption). "The time for *Mashiach* has arrived," he prophesied. He taught that by doing what *Hashem* wants, we can bring the redemption closer.

A trained soldier is a strong soldier.

Armed with your knowledge of Judaism, you can go out there and make the world a better place. Share all that you know with family and friends, helping others grow in their connection to Hashem (G-d) too. And remember that this guide is just the beginning—now it's time to start practicing all of the mitzvot. Who knows, your good deed could be the final one needed to bring *Mashiach* (the Messiah) today!

Glossary

Ach Tzadikim: prayer that reminds us to follow in the path of righteous people

Ahavat Yisrael: commandment to love your fellow Jew

Aleph Bet: the Hebrew alphabet

Amen: something we say after hearing someone else say a blessing

Amidah: a prayer we say 3 times a day that asks G-d to grant us all of our needs (also called Shmoneh Esrei)

Aravot: willow twigs, used with the *lulav* on *Sukkot*

Aron: Ark in the Holy Temple

Avinu: title for the Patriarchs Avraham, Yitzchak, and Yaakov; literally, our father

Bar Mitzvah: 13, the age at which a boy becomes an adult according to Jewish law

Bat Mitzvah: 12, the age at which a girl becomes an adult according to Jewish law

Bechor: firstborn son

Bedikat Chametz: the pre-Passover search for *chametz*

Beit Hamikdash: the Holy Temple in Jerusalem

Bimah: synagogue podium

Birkat Hamazon: a prayer we say after meals during which bread was eaten; also called "Grace After Meals"

Biur Chametz: the pre-Passover burning of the *chametz*

Bnei Yisrael: the Jewish nation; literally, Children of Israel

Boray Nefashot: a prayer we say after eating food for which the blessing of *shehakol*, *ha'aytz* (except the five fruits of Israel), or *ha'adamah* was made

Brachah/Brachot: blessing/s

Brich Rachamana: a prayer we say at the end of a meal in which bread was eaten, when the full prayer cannot be said

Brit Milah: circumcision of a boy at 8 days old

Chalav Yisrael: milk and dairy products that were supervised by Jews

Challah/Challot: braided bread/s we eat on *Shabbat*

Chametz: leavened food forbidden to be eaten or owned on Passover

Chanukah: Hannukah

Chassidim: followers of a *Rebbe*

Chassidut: a Jewish philosophy and way of life founded by the *Baal Shem Tov*, based on the teachings of *Kabbalah*

Chinuch: Jewish education

Chol Hamoed: intermediate days of a holiday, on which some work is permitted

Chukim: *commandments* that are not understandable to us

Chumash: the five books of the *Torah*

Chuppah: Jewish wedding canopy; also the marriage ceremony

Edot: *mitzvot* that commemorate miraculous events

Etrog: citron fruit, used with the lulav on *Sukkot*

Geulah: the Messiah's coming, which will be redemption from the current exile

Glatt Kosher: the title given to meat from animals whose lungs were carefully inspected

Gragger: *Purim* noisemaker

Ha'aytz: blessing made before eating fruits

Ha'adamah: blessing made before eating anything that grew from the ground

Hadasim: myrtle, used with the *lulav* on *Sukkot*

Hagafen: blessing made before drinking wine or grape juice

Haggadah: prayerbook used at the *Seder*

Hakafot: dancing on *Shemini Atzeret* and *Simchat Torah*

Hamotzi: blessing made before eating bread

Hamentash: triangular-shaped cookie we eat on *Purim* (filling reminds us of the hidden miracles that took place)

Hareini: a promise we make to G-d that we will try to love our fellow Jews

Hoshanah Rabbah: seventh day of *Sukkot*

Hashem: G-d, the Creator of the world, our Master and King

Havdalah: a prayer we say at the end of *Shabbat* to separate the holy from the mundane

Imeinu: title for the matriarchs Sarah, Rivkah, Rachel, and Leah; literally, our mother

Kabbalah: deep, abstract secrets of the *Torah*

Kapparot: ceremony performed on the eve of *Yom Kippur*

Ketubah: marriage contract

Ketuvim: writings, the third part of the written *Torah*

Kever Rachel: Rachel's Tomb, located in Bethlehem, Israel

Kibbud Av V'eim: a biblical commandment to honor our mothers and fathers

Kiddush: a prayer we say on wine before the meal on *Shabbat* and *holidays*

Kipah: a head-covering worn by males to remind them that G-d is always watching

Kiyor: wash-basin in the Holy Temple

Kodesh Hakadashim: the innermost and holiest chamber of the Holy Temple; literally, Holy of Holies

Kohen/Kohanim: priest/s

Kosher: food fit for a Jew to eat according to *Torah* law

Lashon Hara: negative talk about other people; gossip

Levi/Levi'im: members of the tribe of Levi, who worked in the Holy Temple

Luchot: Tablets on which the Ten Commandments were engraved

Lulav: date-palm branch, used on *Sukkot*

Ma'arat Hamachpelah: cave located in Chevron, Israel, in which four holy couples are buried

Maariv: the evening prayer service

Mashgiach: a person who supervises the production of food to make sure it is *kosher*

Matanot L'evyonim: charity given on *Purim*

Matzah: unleavened bread, eaten on Passover

Me'ayn Shalosh: a prayer we say after any foods for which the blessings of *mezonot, hagafen,* and *ha'aytz* (for the fruits of Israel) were said

Megillah/Megillat Esther: story of *Purim*, named after its heroine, Queen Esther

Melaveh Malkah: the meal eaten after *Shabbat* ends

Menorah: eight-branched candelabra lit on *Chanukah*

Mezonot: blessing made before eating foods made of these five grains: wheat, barley, spelt, oat, and rye

Mezuzah/Mezuzot: scroll of the *Shema* that is placed on doorways to protect and sanctify our homes

Mikvah: ritual bath

Midrash: commentary on the *Torah*

Minchah: the afternoon prayer service

Minyan: a group of 10 men who gather to pray

Mishkan: portable Temple that the Jews built in the desert

Mishloach Manot: gifts of food sent to friends on *Purim*

Mishnah: six books containing the oral *Torah*

Mishpatim: *mitzvot* that make sense to us

Mishteh: feast

Mitzvah/Mitzvot: Commandment/s given to us by G-d, for us to follow

Mizbe'ach: Altar

Modeh Ani: the prayer we say upon awakening, to thank G-d for returning our soul to our body

Mohel: a rabbi trained to perform circumcisions

Mashiach: the Messiah, our redeemer; also can refer to the era of redemption

Musaf: a prayer added on *Shabbat*, *Rosh Chodesh*, and holidays

Ne'ilah: concluding prayer of *Yom Kippur*

Neshamah: our Jewish soul

Netilat Yadayim: ritual hand-washing done to purify our hands before praying or eating bread

Nevi'im: Prophets; the second part of the written *Torah*

Pareve: food that contains neither meat nor dairy

Parshah/parshiot: weekly *Torah* portion/s

Pesach: Passover, holiday celebrating our redemption from Egyptian slavery

Pesach Sheini: the Second *Pesach*

Pesukim: verses in the *Torah*

Peyot: sidelocks left on a boy after his first haircut

Pidyon Haben: redemption of the firstborn son

Purim: holiday celebrating the Jews' miraculous salvation

Rebbe: Chassidic leader; in Hebrew, this word is an acronym for "head of the Jewish people"

Rosh Chodesh: celebration of the new month

Rosh Hashanah: the Jewish New Year

Sanhedrin: the Jewish Supreme Court

Seder: the Passover ceremonial dinner

Sefardic: of Spanish or Portuguese descent, or Western Asia origin

Sefer Torah: *Torah* scroll

Sefer Hamitzvot: Book of *Commandments*; written by Maimonides

Sefirat Ha'Omer: 49 days of counting from *Pesach* until the giving of the *Torah* on *Shavuot*

Seudah Shelishit: the third meal eaten on *Shabbat*

Shabbat: the seventh day of the week, when we rest, pray, and eat festive meals

Shacharit: the morning prayer service

Shavuot: holiday celebrating the giving of the *Torah*

Shechitah: the laws of slaughtering *kosher* animals

Shechted: slaughtered according to *Torah* law

Shehakol: blessing made before eating foods that aren't made of grain and don't grow on a tree or from the ground

Shehecheyanu: blessing made on special occasions

Shema: a daily prayer in which we declare G-d as One

Shemini Atzeret: holiday after *Sukkot*

Sheyiboneh: a prayer asking G-d to rebuild the Holy Temple right now

Shluchim: messengers, sent by the Lubavitcher Rebbe to spread Judaism

Shmura matzah: handmade *matzah*

Shofar: horn of a ram, blown on *Rosh Hashanah* and *Yom Kippur*

Shul: synagogue

Shulchan: Table in the Holy Temple, which held 12 loaves of bread

Shulchan Aruch: Code of Jewish Law

Siddur: prayerbook

Simchat Torah: holiday of rejoicing with the *Torah*

Sofer: a person who writes holy scrolls like the *Torah* or *mezuzot*

Sukkah/Sukkot: hut/s built for *Sukkot*

Sukkot: holiday of Tabernacles

Taharat Hamishpachah: the laws of family purity

Tallit Gadol: a prayer shawl worn by married men

Tallit Katan: the everyday *tzitzit* that men and boys wear

Tanach: an acronym for its three sections: *Torah, Nevi'im,* and *Ketuvim*

Tanya: the fundamental book of *Chabad Chassidut*

Tashlich: *Rosh Hashanah* service of symbolically throwing sins away to fish

Techiat Hameitim: resurrection of the dead, which will happen in the times of *Mashiach*

Tefillah: prayer

Tefillin: a leather box with a scroll of *Shema* inside that is worn on the arm and head during prayer

Tefillin Shel Rosh: the *tefillin* that goes on the head

Tefillin Shel Yad: the *tefillin* that goes on the arm and hand

Tehillim: book of Psalms, written by King David

Teshuvah: repentance to G-d; literally, "return"

Teivah: Noah's Ark

Torah: a guidebook for life given to the Jews by G-d through Moses

Tzadik/Tzadikim: righteous people who do not sin

Tzedakah: money or other assistance given to people in need

Tzitzit: an undergarment with knotted strings on each corner, also called *tallit katan*, worn by boys and men

Tzivos Hashem: the Army of G-d

Tzniut: modesty in thought, speech, and action

Upsherinish: first cutting of a boy's hair, at the age of 3

V'al Hanissim: special prayer said on *Chanukah* and *Purim*

Yad Hachazakah: a series on *Torah* law written by Maimonides; literally, "The Mighty Arm"

Yeshivah: school of *Torah* study

Yetzer Hara: bad Inclination

Yetzer Tov: good Inclination

Yom Kippur: the Day of Atonement; the holiest day of the year

Yom Tov: a Jewish holiday

Zohar: holy book of mysticism and *Kabbalah*, written by Rabbi Shimon bar Yochai

Merkos L'Inyonei Chinuch
Rabbi Moshe Kotlarsky

Tzivos Hashem
Rabbi Yerachmiel Benjaminson
Rabbi Sholom Ber Baumgarten
Rabbi Zalman Glick
Rabbi Shimmy Weinbaum

Merkos Suite 302
Rabbi Mendy Kotlarsky
Rabbi Berl Frankel
Rabbi Duvi Feldman

CKids
Rabbi Zalmy Loewenthal
Chaya Loewenthal
Mussie Weiss

Public Relations
Bentzi Sasson

Programming
Yehoshua Berkowicz
Andy Dear
Shaya Smetana
Naftoli Rapoport

*Special thanks to Rabbis
Michoel Alburkerk and Dovid
Sholom Pape, whose work on
the original Tzivos Hashem
handbook laid the groundwork
for this project.*

Living Jewish
Chava Leiba Witkes

Review Panel
Rabbi Levi Brashevitzky
Rabbi Sender Engel
Rabbi Zalman Kudan
Rabbi Levi Raskin
Rabbi Shmuel Vaisfiche
Rabbi Boruch Lesches

Editorial Team
Chana Sarale Krasnjanski
Shterna Karp
Mushka Gopin
Miriam Hertzel

Proofreading
Yonit Tanenbaum
Shanna Fuld
Emily Pysczynski
Rabbi Natan Grunblatt

Design
Chana Cohen
Chaya M Raskin
Rochel Barber
Levi Groner
Esty Raskin
Spotlight Design

Transliteration
Rabbi Shmuel Rabin
Rabbi Zalman Goldstein

Text and Translation
Kehot Publication Society
Tzivos Hashem Weiss Siddur

Art
Stelian Dobrescu
Rabbi Fishel Jacobs, pgs. 160-161
Nikolinka Vukadinova

Photos
Bentzi Sasson, CTeen. pg. 94
Shmuli Evers, pg. 143
Chana Blumes, pg.149
Rabbi Aron Rabin
Chaim Perl, pg. 139